UNDERSTANDING
Everyday Australian

Book One

*A focus on spoken language
with language reviews, exercises and answers*

Susan Boyer

Boyer Educational Resources 1998
Reprinted 2000, 2001, 2004, 2007, 2008, 2009, 2011, 2015, 2017

Boyer Educational Resources
PO Box 255, Glenbrook 2773
Phone/fax (02) 47391538
www.boyereducation.com.au

© Boyer Educational Resources 1998
Reprinted 2000, 2001, 2004, 2007, 2008, 2009, 2011, 2015, 2017

Cover illustrations & illustrations throughout this book are by Matthew J Larwood.

Acknowledgements

I would like to express my thanks to the following people for their contribution to the final presentation of this book:

Thank you to Matthew Larwood, for his patient consultation regarding the illustrations throughout the book. I am grateful also to the teachers at Nepean College of TAFE who trialed the material contained in this book and suggested improvements. Also I would like to thank my friend, Ingrid, for her participation in the audio recording which accompanies this book. Thank you to Ann Baker for her review of this book and her constructive comments. I am thankful also for the encouragement and professional advice I received from my father, Vince Willder. To my son, Clinton, I would like to say thank you for your careful proof-reading and editing work, as well as your contribution to the accompanying audio recording. And finally, to my precious husband, Len, who spent many hours proof reading, editing and formatting this book, I want to say thank you for your support, encouragement and interest in my work. I am also indebted to you for your great ideas which became incorporated into the final presentation of the book.

The clipart images used herein were obtained from IMSI's MasterClips Collection,
1895 Francisco Blvd. East, San Rafael, CA 94901-5506, USA..
The kookaburra clipart was obtained from Australian Graphics Selection, New Horizons, Armidale. Australia.

National Library of Australia
Cataloguing-in-Publication data:

Boyer, Susan
Understanding Everyday Australian : A focus on spoken language with language reviews, exercises and answers.

ISBN 978 0 9585395 00 .

1. English language - Spoken English - Australia - Textbooks for foreign speakers.
2. English language - Spoken English - Australia - Problems, exercises, etc. I.
Boyer, Leonard, 1951- . II. Title.

428.34

© Boyer Educational Resources: Phone/Fax 02 4739 1538
   www.boyereducation.com.au

For information on copying material in this book, please contact: Susan Boyer   Ph: 0407274380
          or
CAL (Copyright Agency Limited)
Level 15, 233 Castlereagh Street, Sydney 2000
Phone 02 93947600
www.copyright.com.au   email: services@copyright.com.au

DEAR ENGLISH LANGUAGE STUDENT,

Welcome to *Understanding Everyday Australian - Book One*. This book, along with its accompanying audio recording, has been designed to help you to understand English as it is spoken in everyday situations in Australia. As a student of English as a second language, I am sure you are aware of the difference between the formally presented language of the textbook and the speech you hear, outside the language classroom, in your daily activities and conversations with Australians.

As well as introducing over 200 commonly heard everyday expressions, the book focuses on other aspects of spoken English which make it difficult for learners to understand. For example, you will practise listening for the use of *contractions* (eg. *I'll* rather than *I will*.) You will also learn how *stress* (some words being spoken more loudly and clearly than others) and *intonation* (the rise and fall in the voice) are used in spoken English. You will also learn social conventions involved in everyday situations such as making a telephone call, dealing with service people and informal introductions.

I sincerely hope you enjoy and benefit from using *Understanding Everyday Australian.*

Susan Boyer

ABOUT THIS BOOK

Understanding Everyday Australian has been designed so that you can work through it alone, without the help of a teacher, or in a classroom situation with other students. The book contains nine units of work, each based on a conversation about a particular topic. The units are divided into *six parts* that have been designed to introduce unfamiliar language, *step by step,* in a gradual and systematic way. The layout of the book is as follows:

Part 1 - Focus on listening for general understanding

Part 1 introduces the topic and invites you to listen to an everyday conversation and answer a few general questions by putting a tick next to the correct answers. You will be listening for *general* understanding of the conversation only. (You will not need to understand every word). This is an important step as it will help you to realise that it's not always necessary to hear every word to understand the general meaning of a conversation. In some units, you are asked to check words in a dictionary, so have a dictionary nearby when you are studying.

Part 2 - Focus on reading & finding the meaning

In this section, you will *read* Conversation 1 as you listen again. When you have finished listening, your task is to *compare Conversation 1 with Conversation 2* (which will be next to Conversation 1). Conversation 1 contains the everyday expressions and Conversation 2 contains an interpretation of the expressions in Conversation 1. This section will help you to learn the *meaning* of the everyday expressions.

Part 3 - Focus on listening for detail

Now you will listen to Conversation 1 again and write in the missing words in the spaces as you hear them. Don't worry about spelling as this exercise focuses on your *listening skills*. Listen to the conversation as many times as you like, then check your answers (and spelling) by comparing what you have written with Conversation 1.

Part 4 - Focus on writing for reinforcement

This section reinforces (strengthens) your memory as you listen once more to Conversation 1 and tick the newly learnt everyday expressions on the list as you hear them. Then you are asked to look at the list of expressions (all taken from Conversation 1) and try to remember their meaning. Write in the ones that you can remember, then check your answers by reading Conversation 1 again or checking the reference list at the back of the book. This may seem like hard work but *writing* the meanings of the newly learnt expressions is a useful way of reinforcing what you have just heard and read.

Part 5 - Focus on revision

Now it's time to test yourself and see what you have learnt by trying the language review. In this section, you are asked to use the newly learnt expressions in a different context. Firstly, you are asked to complete sentences with an appropriate expression and then complete a crossword. The answers to the crosswords can be found in the back of the book.

Part 6 - Focus on spoken language

This section focuses on other aspects of spoken English that make it difficult for learners to understand native speakers. Each unit highlights and explains a particular aspect of pronunciation, sentence structure or conversation strategy which was used by the speakers in Conversation 1 of that unit. In this section, there will be exercises for you to complete to help you understand, learn and remember.

Language Reviews

After Unit 3, Unit 6 and Unit 9, you will find a language review which consists of the recently introduced expressions and pictures for you to match together. This will help you to see how much you have remembered. Don't worry if you make a mistake - you are still learning.

IMPORTANT NOTE TO STUDENTS

Please be aware that the meaning of colloquial language is ***very dependent on the context or situation in which it is used***. *'Understanding Everyday Australian'* has been designed to ***introduce and explain*** the meaning of colloquial expressions used by English speakers in the everyday situations presented in this book. However, because colloquial expressions can have different meanings in different situations, it is not advisable that students of Australian English immediately begin using the newly introduced expressions indiscriminately. It would be much better to spend time listening, recognising, and understanding the correct meaning of expressions in different situations ***before you use them*** in your conversations.

In this regard, the author and publisher of this book will not be responsible to any person, with regard to the misuse of language, caused directly or indirectly by the information presented in this book.

UNDERSTANDING EVERYDAY AUSTRALIAN – BOOK ONE

CONTENTS

UNIT 1

STARTING SOMETHING NEW

We all learn new things throughout our lives - sometimes because we want to and sometimes because we have to. How do you feel about learning new things? Most people have "mixed feelings" about starting new things. This means they often feel nervous and excited at the same time.

Listen to this conversation between friends who are talking about starting something new. (Unit 1 on your audio recording.) The conversation contains many colloquial or everyday expressions which will be explained later in the unit - so don't worry if you don't understand every word. This time you are only listening for a general understanding of the topic. As you listen, tick the correct answers below. (There may be more than one correct answer.) When you have finished you can check your answers on page 83.

1) Chris is telephoning Lee to ask about:

> a) her new job
>
> b) a new language course
>
> c) a new hobby

2) Lee suggests that Chris should enrol in:

> a) an accountancy course
>
> b) a computer course
>
> c) a cooking course

3) Chris says:

> a) he is too old to learn new things
>
> b) he already knows how to do it
>
> c) he will enquire about a course this week

> **Now we'll look at the everyday expressions used in the conversation - turn to the next page.**

CONVERSATION 1 (with everyday expressions)

Read this conversation as you listen to the audio tape. Do you know what the _underlined_ words mean? They are colloquial or 'everyday' expressions.

Chris: Hello Lee. It's Chris here. I thought I'd **_give you a buzz_** and see how you're **_getting on_** in your new job.

Lee: Oh hi Chris. It's good to hear from you. I'm **_going great guns_** now thanks. I had a few **_hassles_** at first - you know everything was different - but now I've **_got the hang of it._** In the first week I thought the job **_was beyond_** me. I **_couldn't make head nor tail of_** the accounts system but I **_stuck at it_** and I'm **_getting into the swing of things_** now.

Chris: **_Good for you_**!

Lee: Thanks. What've you been **_up to_** anyway?

Chris: Not much. I should **_take a leaf out of your book_** and get some training and go for a better job.

Lee: Yes, you should. Why don't you do a computer course?

Chris: I don't really like the idea of studying again - it's so long since I left school. I **_haven't the foggiest idea_** about computers. I mean, what if everyone else in the class **_catches on_** quicker than me. I'm getting a bit old to learn new **_tricks_**.

Lee: Oh**_, come off it!_** **_Heaps_** of people study as adults these days. Everyone in the class will be **_in the same boat._** **_Go on_** Chris! Once you start, I'm sure you'll soon **_get the hang_** of it.

Chris: OK. You've **_talked me into it_**. I'll enquire about courses this week.

Lee: Good on you! Look, I'd better get back to work now - we're pretty busy today but I'll call you next week to see how you're getting on.

Chris: OK. I'll talk to you then. Thanks for the encouragement! **_Catch you later._**

Lee: **_Hooroo_**.......and good luck!

Now let's see what these expressions mean - look at the next page.

CONVERSATION 2 (explanation of everyday expressions)

Compare Conversation 1 with Conversation 2 -You will see that some of the words are different but the meaning is the same in both conversations. Find the underlined words in Conversation 1, then underline the words with the same meaning in Conversation 2. For example: *give you a buzz* (Conversation 1) = *call you on the telephone* (Conversation 2)

Chris: Hello Lee. It's Chris here. I thought I'd <u>call you on the telephone</u> and see how you are progressing in your new job.

Lee: Oh hi Chris. It's good to hear from you. I'm progressing very well now thanks. I had a few difficulties at first - you know everything was different - but now I understand what to do. In the first week I thought the job was too difficult for me. I couldn't understand anything about the accounts system but I kept trying and I'm becoming familiar with the usual way of doing things now.

Chris: Congratulations!

Lee: Thanks. What've you been doing anyway?

Chris: Not much. I should copy your good example and get some training and go for a better job.

Lee: Yes, you should. Why don't you do a computer course?

Chris: I don't really like the idea of studying again - it's so long since I left school. I haven't any knowledge about computers. What if everyone else in the class learns/understands quicker than me. I'm getting a bit old to learn new ways of doing things.

Lee: Oh I don't agree with you! A lot of people study as adults these days. Everyone in the class will be in the same situation. You should do it, Chris! Once you start, I'm sure you'll soon understand what to do..

Chris: OK. You've shown me good reasons why I should do what you suggest. I'll enquire about courses this week.

Lee: Good on you! Look, I'd better get back to work now - we're pretty busy today but I'll call you next week to see how you're getting on.

Chris: OK. I'll talk to you then. Thanks for the encouragement! Goodbye.

Lee: Goodbye......and good luck!

Now to become familiar with the everyday expressions, practise reading CONVERSATION 1 aloud with a partner.

Listen to the conversation again and fill in the missing words. You may have to listen more than once. (Don't worry about your spelling as this exercise focuses on listening skills - you can check your spelling later.)

Chris: Hello Lee. It's Chris here. I thought I'd **_give you a_** _____ and see how you are **_getting on_** in your new job.

Lee: Oh hi Chris. It's good to hear from you. I'm **_going great_** _____ now thanks. I had a few _____ at first, you know everything was different - but now I've **_got the_** _____ **_of it._** In the first week I thought the job **_was beyond_** me. I **_couldn't make_** _____ **_nor_** _____ **_of_** the accounts system but I **_stuck at it_** and I'm **_getting into_** **_the_** _____ **_of things_** now.

Chris: **_Good for you_**!

Lee: Thanks. What've you been **_up to_** anyway?

Chris: Not much. I should **_take a_** _____ **_out of your_** _____ and get some training and go for a better job.

Lee: Yes, you should. Why don't you do a computer course?

Chris: I don't really like the idea of studying again - it's so long since I left school. I **_haven't the_** _____ **_idea_** about computers. I mean what if everyone else in the class **_catches_** _____ quicker than me. I'm getting a bit old to learn new _____.

Lee: Oh, **_come off it!_** _____ of people study as adults these days. Everyone in the class will be **_in the same_** _____. **_Go on_** Chris! Once you start, I'm sure you'll soon get the hang of it.

Chris: OK. You've **_talked me_** _____ **_it_** . I'll enquire about courses this week.

Lee: Good on you! Look, I'd better get back to work now - we're pretty busy today but I'll call you next week to see how you're getting on.

Chris: OK. I'll talk to you then. Thanks for the encouragement! _____ **_you later._**

Lee: **_Hooroo_**......and good luck!

> **Now check your answers by comparing this page with CONVERSATION 1**

In order to become more familiar with these new everyday expressions:

1) Listen to Conversation 1 again and tick the boxes ☐ next to the expressions as you hear them.
2) After the conversation has finished, write in the definitions you can remember. (Some have been done for you as examples.)
3) Check your answers by turning to page 90.

☐ give (someone) a buzz...

☐ getting on ....*progressing*...

☐ going great guns..

☐ hassles..

☐ get the hang of it.......................... *understand what to do*.....................................

☐ beyond (someone)..

☐ *not* make head or tail of (something).....*not understand anything about (something)*.............

☐ stick at it...

☐ get into the swing of things...

☐ Good for you!...

☐ What've you been up to?....................*What've you been doing?*..................................

☐ take a leaf out of (someone's) book..

☐ *not* have the foggiest idea about (something)..

☐ catch on...

☐ (new) tricks..

☐ Come off it!..

☐ heaps..

☐ in the same boat..

☐ Go on!...*You should do it!*..

☐ talk into... *show good reasons for doing something*................

☐ catch you later!...

☐ Hooroo...

LANGUAGE NOTE:

The expressions, "**not** have the foggiest idea", "**not** make head nor tail", are usually expressed in the negative form. (i.e. have _not_, can _not_)

LANGUAGE REVIEW

Complete the sentences, choosing from the everyday expressions which are listed below. You can use the clues in brackets ( ) at the end of each sentence to help you. Then complete the crossword using the everyday expressions you have written. The first one has been done as an example.

head nor tail	stick at	~~got the hang~~	leaf	catch on	great guns
heaps	swing	beyond	buzz	same boat	

ACROSS

1) I didn't understand this game before but now I've **got the hang** of it. (understand what to do)
3) This textbook is _____ me. (too difficult for)
5) I can't make _____ ____ _____ of this grammar book. (understand anything)
7) There're always _____ of people at the beach in Summer. (a lot of)
9) Everyone who has started their life again in a new country is in the _____ ____ .
   (same situation)

DOWN

2) It's easier to _____ ___ to new things if you relax and enjoy learning. (learn/understand)
4) "How are you going in your new course?" "I'm going _____ _____ thanks." (doing well)
6) I'm going to take a _____ out of your book and practise English everyday too. (copy your good example)
8) I practise English everyday and now I'm getting into the _____ of things. (becoming familiar with the usual way of doing things)
10) I'll give you a _____tonight and we can make arrangements for tomorrow. (call on the telephone)
12) This course is difficult but I'm going to _____ ___ it. I'm sure it will get easier. (keep trying)

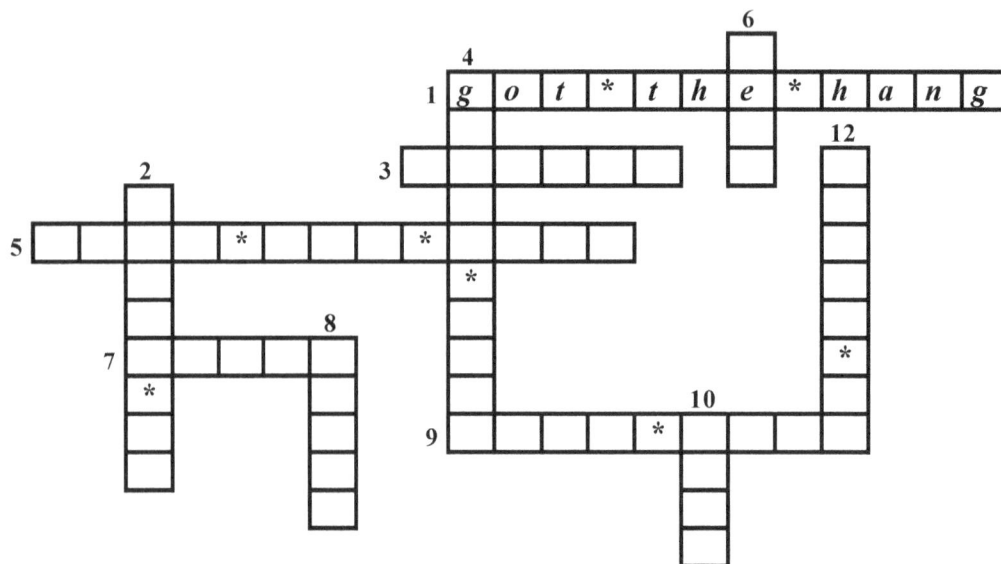

(Answers: page 83)

FOCUS ON SPOKEN LANGUAGE

Some words or groups of words are difficult to hear in English because when we speak we use "contractions" or short forms of words. For example, instead of saying, "I would..." we say "I'd..."

Listen to *Conversation 1* again and circle the contractions used in the conversation (page 3) as you hear them. Listen to the way the contractions are pronounced. How many contractions did you find? (Answers p. 83)

PRACTICE

Write the contracted form of these groups of words that have been used in Conversation 1. Notice the correct position for the apostrophe (').

		Write your answers here.
For example:	I would..	*I'd*
	I am...	_____
	I have...	_____
	could not...	_____
	do not...	_____
	have not..	_____
	They will...	_____
	You have..	_____
	I had..	_____
	they are..	_____

FOCUS ON TELEPHONE LANGUAGE

When we call people we know on the telephone, we often begin the conversation by saying "Hello, this is Susan." or "Hello, it's Susan here." We never say, "I am Susan."
Notice how Chris introduced his call to Lee in Conversation 1.

If it's a business call, we would introduce ourselves, using our surname. For example: "Hello, this is Susan Boyer......" or if it's our first call, "Hello, my name is Susan Boyer......"

UNIT 2

TALKING ABOUT THE FAMILY

This conversation contains colloquial or everyday expressions relating to family life. These will be explained later in the unit so don't worry if you don't understand every word of the conversation. This time you are only listening for gist or general understanding of the topic. Listen to the conversation between friends (Unit 2 on your audio recording.) and decide which of the photographs on the opposite page they are talking about? (Answers: page 83)

Before you listen to the conversation again, check these words in a dictionary if you are not familiar with their meaning.

in-laws	characteristics	relationship	(cultural) background	tolerant

Listen to the conversation again and tick the correct answer below. You may need to listen more than once. When you have finished, you can check your answers on page 83.

1) How many sons does Jean have?

    a) two

    b) three

    c) four

2) What is David's health problem?

    a) an eye problem

    b) a hearing problem

    c) a heart problem

3) What has caused the problem between Jean's daughters-in-law ?

    a) business problems

    b) cultural differences

    c) health problems

Now we'll look at the everyday expressions used in the conversation - turn to the next page.

CONVERSATION 1 (with everyday expressions)

Read this conversation as you listen to the audio tape. Do you know what the _underlined_ words mean? They are "colloquial" or everyday expressions.

Merv: Are these your sons, Jean? I haven't seen them for **_ages_**.

Jean: Yes, that photo was taken a few months ago.

Merv: John hasn't changed a bit. He's **_the image of_** his father, isn't he?

Jean: Yes, he is. He **_takes after_** his father, that's for sure.

Merv: **_I reckon!_**

Jean: He's **_followed in his father's footsteps_** too and works in the family importing business. He's living overseas at the moment.

Merv: Oh really? How does he like it?

Jean: It was difficult for him at first because he had to **_start from scratch_**, you know, finding somewhere to live and making new friends. He's **_settled in_** now though and he loves it.

Merv: Oh, good - Give him **_my best_** when you talk to him. And how is David?

Jean: Well I'm sorry to say, he hasn't been very well. He's been having problems with his heart. We're very worried about him because heart disease **_runs in_** our family you know.

Merv: **_Fair dinkum?_** I didn't know that.

Jean: Yes, my younger brother **_passed away_** last year after a heart attack.

Merv: Oh, I'm very sorry to hear that, Jean. He wasn't very old, was he?

Jean: No, he wasn't - only thirty four. At least David knows about the problem and he can look after himself.

Merv: Mm. And do the boys **_keep in touch_**. I remember they used to **_be very close_**.

Jean: Yes they do - but not as much as before they were married. Their wives don't **_get on_**, so it makes it a bit **_sticky_**, you know.

Merv: Really? That's no good! In-laws can be a problem sometimes, can't they?

Jean: Yes, they can sometimes. This problem is because they're from different cultural backgrounds.

Merv: Fair dinkum?

Jean: Mm. It's **_a tough one_** because we **_brought up_** the boys to be tolerant about other cultures and to **_get on with_** everyone.

Merv: Well let's hope their ideas **_rub off on_** their wives.

Jean: Yes, let's hope so.

Now let's see what these expressions mean - look at the next page.

CONVERSATION 2 (explanation of everyday expressions)

Compare Conversation 1 with Conversation 2 -You will see that some of the words are different but the meaning is the same in both conversations. Find the underlined words in Conversation 1, then underline the words with the same meaning in Conversation 2. For example: ages (Conversation 1) = a long time (Conversation 2)

Merv: Are these your sons Jean? I haven't seen them for a long time.

Jean: Yes, that photo was taken a few months ago.

Merv: John hasn't changed a bit. He's the same as his father in appearance, isn't he?

Jean: Yes, he is. He is similar to his father, that's for sure.

Merv: I agree!

Jean: He's done the same as his father did too and works in the family importing business. He's living overseas at the moment.

Merv: Oh really? How does he like it?

Jean: It was difficult for him at first because he had to start from the beginning without help, you know, finding somewhere to live and making new friends. He's become established now though and he loves it.

Merv: Oh, good. - Give him my best wishes when you talk to him. And how is David?

Jean: Well, I'm sorry to say, he hasn't been very well. He's been having problems with his heart. We're very worried about him because heart disease is a common characteristic in our family, you know.

Merv: Really? I didn't know that.

Jean: Yes, my younger brother died last year after a heart attack.

Merv: Oh, I'm sorry to hear that, Jean. He wasn't very old, was he?

Jean: No, he wasn't - only thirty four. At least David knows about the problem and he can look after himself.

Merv: Mm. And do the boys communicate regularly? I remember they used to have a very good relationship.

Jean: Yes they do - but not as much as before they were married. Their wives don't like each other, so it makes it a bit difficult, you know.

Merv: Really? That's not good! In-laws can be a problem sometimes, can't they?

Jean: Yes, they can sometimes. This problem is because they are from different cultural backgrounds.

Merv: Really?

Jean: Mm. It's a difficult problem because we trained and educated the boys to be tolerant about other cultures and to be friendly with everyone.

Merv: Well let's hope their ideas are transferred to their wives.

Jean: Yes, let's hope so.

> **Now to become familiar with the everyday expressions, practise reading CONVERSATION 1 aloud with a partner.**

Listen to the conversation again and fill in the missing words. You may have to listen more than once. Don't worry about your spelling as this exercise focuses on listening skills.

Merv: Are these your sons Jean? I haven't seen them for _____.

Jean: Yes, that photo was taken a few months ago.

Merv: John hasn't changed a bit. He's **_the_____ _of_** his father, isn't he?

Jean: Yes, he is. He **_takes_____** his father, that's for sure.

Merv: **_I reckon!_**

Jean: He's _____ **_in his father's footsteps_** too and works in the family importing business. He's living overseas at the moment.

Merv: Oh really? How does he like it?

Jean: It was difficult for him at first because he had to **_start from_____**, you know, finding somewhere to live and making new friends. He's **_settled in_** now though and he loves it.

Merv: Oh good, - Give him **_my_____** when you talk to him. And how is David?

Jean: Well I'm sorry to say, he hasn't been very well. He's been having problems with his heart. We're very worried about him because heart disease _____ **_in_** our family you know.

Merv: _____ **_dinkum?_** I didn't know that.

Jean: Yes, my younger brother _____ **_away_** last year after a heart attack.

Merv: Oh, I'm very sorry to hear that, Jean. He wasn't very old, was he?

Jean: No, he wasn't - only thirty four. At least David knows about the problem and he can look after himself.

Merv: Mm. And do the boys **_keep in_____?** I remember they used to **_be very close_**.

Jean: Yes they do - but not as much as before they were married. Their wives don't _____ **_on_**, so it makes it a bit _____, you know.

Merv: Really? That's no good! In-laws can be a problem sometimes, can't they?

Jean: Yes, they can sometimes. This problem's because they're from different cultural backgrounds.

Merv: Fair dinkum?

Jean: Mm. It's **_a tough_____** because we **_brought_____** the boys to be tolerant about other cultures and to _____ **_on with_** everyone.

Merv: Well let's hope their ideas **_rub_____ on_** their wives.

> Now check your answers by comparing this page with CONVERSATION 1

In order to become more familiar with these new everyday expressions,

1) Listen to Conversation 1 again and tick the boxes ☐ next to the expressions as you hear them.
2) After the conversation has finished, write in the definitions you can remember. (Some have been done for you as examples.)
3) Check your answers by turning to page 91.

☐ for ages..

☐ the image of (someone)...

☐ take after..

☐ I reckon!...

☐ follow in (someone's) footsteps..

☐ start from scratch...

☐ be settled in...

☐ give (someone) my best..

☐ runs in the family..

☐ fair dinkum?...*really?*..

☐ passed away...

☐ keep in touch..

☐ be very close.......................................*have a good relationship*...................

☐ not get on..*to not like (another person)*...............

☐ sticky (situation)...

☐ a tough one...

☐ bring up (children)..

☐ get on with...

☐ rub off on...*to transfer (a habit, idea) to another person*..........

CULTURAL NOTE: It's always difficult to know what to say when someone tells us that a member of their family has **passed away** (died). An appropriate answer in English is: "I'm very sorry to hear that."

LANGUAGE NOTE: ***Fair dinkum*** is an Australian expression which generally means "true" or "honest". It can be used to describe someone or something. e.g. "He's a fair dinkum friend." or "It's a fair dinkum business deal."- or as in Conversation 1 of this unit, it can be used to mean, "Really?", "Is that true?"

LANGUAGE REVIEW

Complete the sentences, choosing from the everyday expressions which are listed below. You can use the clues in brackets ( ) at the end of each sentence to help you. Then complete the crossword using the everyday expressions you have written. The first one has been done as an example.

~~brought up~~	get on	sticky	runs in	passed away	ages
take after	settle in	keep in touch	start from scratch		

ACROSS

1) I was ***brought*** ***up*** by my parents to believe that honesty and hard work are very important. (trained and educated in the family)
3) I haven't had a holiday for _____.(a long time)
5) When we moved here, it took us a year to _____ ___and make new friends. (become established)
7) When we moved overseas, we had to _____ _____ _____ because we didn't know anyone. (start from the beginning without help)
9) Mary and Bob are divorced, so their son's wedding could be a bit _____. (difficult)

DOWN

2) My next door neighbours don't ____ ___ . (like each other)
4) Poor eyesight _____ ___our family so most of us have to wear glasses. (is a common characteristic)
6) I _____ _____ my mother but my sister takes after my father. (am similar to)
8) My grandfather _____ _____ before I was born. (died)
10)Do you_____ ____ _____ with your friends from school? (communicate regularly)

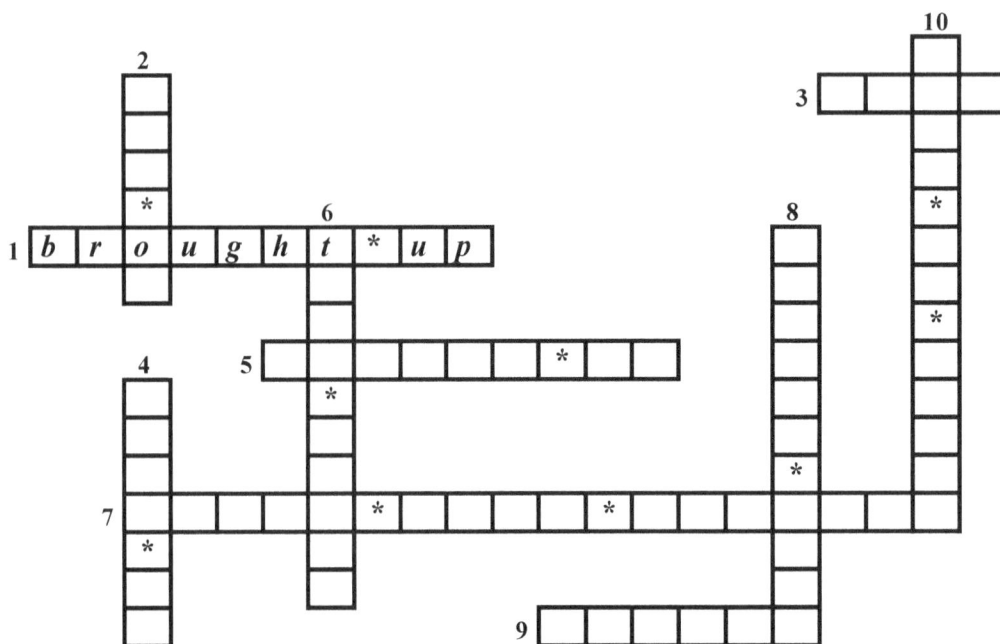

(Answers: page 83)

FOCUS ON SPOKEN LANGUAGE

In spoken English, we sometimes use 'question tags' at the end of a sentence to make it more conversational. For example, "It's very hot today, _**isn't it?**_" (The last part, _**"isn't it?"**_ is called the question tag).

- Look at Conversation 1 of this unit again (page 11).
- Find Merv's statements with a question tag at the end.
- Write them in the space below. You should be able to find three sentences with question tags.
- Look at the short replies that Jean gives and write them next to Merv's sentences. Jean's first reply has been written for you. (Answers: page 84)

MERV'S STATEMENTS (with question tag)　　　　　　**_JEAN'S REPLY_**

1) _____ _Yes, he is._

2) _____ _____

3) _____ _____

NOTICE THE PATTERN

Statement	**Question tag**	**Short reply**
He _is_ the image of his father,	_**isn't** he?_	_Yes, he **is.**_

If the first part of the sentence has a **_positive_** verb, the question tag is **_negative._**
If the first part of the sentence has a **_negative_** verb, the question tag is **_positive._**
When the speaker is using a question tag to be conversational, the reply agrees
with the first part of the sentence. For example:

He _**wasn't**_ very old,	_**was** he?_	_No, he **wasn't.**_

Practise adding a question tag to these statements. (Firstly, notice the verb in the first part of the sentence - is it positive or negative?) Then add a short reply. (Answers: page 84)

a) **Cars can be expensive,**.......................... _____? _____

b) **It's cold today,**................................._____? _____

c) **This classroom isn't very big,**................_____? _____

d) **This food is delicious,**........................... _____? _____

USING QUESTION TAGS
When we use question tags to be friendly or conversational, we usually aren't asking for information - we already know the answer.
For example: "Christmas will be here soon, won't it?" "Yes, it certainly will."
　　　　　　 "It's not very busy today, is it?"　　　　 "No, it isn't."
Don't worry if this structure is still a little confusing. Just listen to people when you are shopping, at work or watching television and become more aware of how we use question tags. The more you listen, the more familiar you'll become with everyday expressions.
　　　　　(There will also be revision on 'question tags' in a later unit of this book.)

UNIT 3

TALKING ABOUT THE NEIGHBOURS

I'm fed up with my neighbours!
Their place is a real eyesore!

In English there is a saying, "It takes all kinds to make a world" (sometimes we say, "It takes all kinds......".) This means that every person is different and we have to accept their differences. However, sometimes that's not so easy when we have problems with other people, especially neighbours!

Listen to this conversation between two neighbours who are talking about their other neighbours. (Unit 3 on your audio recording.) The conversation contains many colloquial or everyday expressions which will be explained later in the unit - so don't worry if you don't understand every word. This time you are only listening for gist or general understanding of the topic. As you listen, tick the correct answers below. You can check your answers on page 84.

1) At the beginning of the conversation, Jane is

        a) very happy.

        b) not very happy.

2) During the conversation, Jane says she

        a) doesn't like any of her neighbours.

        b) likes her neighbours on both sides of her house.

        c) likes the neighbours who live on one side of her house but doesn't like the neighbours on the other side.

3) During the conversation, Bob says

        a) he hasn't met his new neighbours yet.

        b) he has met his new neighbours.

4) Jane says that the person who lives in number 5

        a) likes gardening.

        b) is probably watching TV.

        c) is probably watching her and Bob.

Now we'll look at the everyday expressions used in the conversation - turn to the next page.

CONVERSATION 1 (with everyday expressions)

Read this conversation as you listen to the audio recording. Do you know what the _underlined_ words mean? They are colloquial or 'everyday' expressions.

Bob: Hi Jane. How are you?

Jane: I'm feeling a bit **_out of sorts_** this morning, Bob. I **_didn't sleep a wink_** last night. The people next door were making **_a racket_** again until **_all hours_**. They **_couldn't care less_** about anyone else. I'm **_fed up_** with the situation but I just don't know what to do about it.

Bob: Why don't you **_go crook on_** them.

Jane: Oh, I don't want to **_make waves_**. They might get **_stroppy_**, you know. If I go crook, they could even get **_aggro_**. You know, I mean.....

Bob: Yes, I know what you mean - they seem a bit **_way-out_**.

Jane: It's not just the noise..... Just look at their place. ... it's **_a real eyesore._**
I wish they were like my other neighbours. They're **_terrific_**! Their place is **_spot on_** and they're so **_easy to get on with_**. They've lived there for years and we've never had any **_hassles._** But these other people .....Oh I don't know what to do. By the way, how're your new neighbours Bob? Have you met them yet?

Bob: No I haven't...... but they seem to be a bit **_standoffish_**. I've tried to say hello but they **_give me the cold shoulder_**. So I think they're **_stuck up_**, if you ask me.

Jane: Oh dear....well I suppose it's better than having **_a sticky beak_**, like Mrs. Jones, living next door.

Bob: Mrs. Jones?

Jane: Yes... you know **_the busybody_** from number five. She knows everything that's **_going on_** in the street..... In fact she's probably watching us right now.

Bob: Yeah probably.

Jane: Oh well, it takes all kinds to make a world.

Now let's see what these expressions mean - look at the next page.

CONVERSATION 2 - (explanation of everyday expressions)

Compare Conversation 1 with Conversation 2 -You will see that some of the words are different but the meaning is the same in both conversations. Find the underlined words in Conversation 1, then underline the words with the same meaning in Conversation 2. For example: <u>out of sorts</u> (Conversation 1) = <u>unhappy</u> (Conversation 2)

Bob: Hi Jane. How are you?

Jane: I'm feeling a bit <u>unhappy</u> this morning, Bob. I didn't sleep at all last night. The people next door were making a lot of noise again till very late at night. They don't care about anyone else. I'm very unhappy with the situation but I just don't know what to do about it.

Bob: Why don't you tell them that you are displeased with them.

Jane: Oh, I don't want to cause trouble. They might get angry/ difficult to deal with, you know. If I tell them I'm displeased, they could even get aggressive. You know, I mean.....

Bob: Yes, I know what you mean - they seem a bit strange/unusual.

Jane: It's not just the noise.......Just look at their place......it's a very unpleasant place to look at. I wish they were like my other neighbours. They are excellent! Their place is perfect and they are so friendly. They've lived there for years and we've never had any problems. But these other people......Oh I don't know what to do. By the way, how are your new neighbours Bob? Have you met them yet?

Bob: No, I haven't......but they seem to be a bit unfriendly. I've tried to say hello, but they deliberately ignore me. So I think they believe they are superior to me, if you ask me.

Jane: Oh dear........ well I suppose it's better than having a person who is always watching what other people are doing, like Mrs. Jones, living next door.

Bob: Mrs Jones?

Jane: Yes....you know, the interfering person from number five. She knows everything that is happening in the street.....In fact she's probably watching us right now.

Bob: Yes probably.

Jane: Oh well, it takes all kinds to make a world.

> Now to become familiar with the everyday expressions, practise reading CONVERSATION 1 aloud with a partner.

Listen to the conversation again and fill in the missing words. Don't worry about your spelling, as this exercise focuses on your listening skills - you can check your spelling later. (You may have to listen more than once.)

Bob: Hi Jane. How are you?

Jane: I'm feeling a bit _____*of sorts* this morning, Bob. I ***didn't sleep a***_____ last night. The

        people next door were making ***a racket*** again until _____ ***hours***. They ***couldn't care less***

        about anyone else. I'm ***fed***_____ with the situation but I just don't know what to do

        about it.

Bob: Why don't you ***go crook***_____them.

Jane: Oh, I don't want to ***make***_____. They might get ***stroppy***, you know. If I go crook, they

        could ***get***_____. You know, I mean.....

Bob: Yeah. I know what you mean.... They seem a bit _____***out***.

Jane: It's not just the noise..... Just look at their place. ... it's ***a real***_____***sore.***

        I wish they were like my other neighbours. They're ***terrific***! Their place is ***spot***_____and

        they are so ***easy to***_____***on with***. They've lived there for years and we've never had any

        hassles. But these other people.....Oh I don't know what to do. By the way, how're your

        new neighbours Bob? Have you met them yet?

Bob: No I haven't..... but they seem to be ***a bit standoffish***. I've tried to say hello but they

        give me the_____***shoulder***. So I think they're ***stuck***_____, if you ask me.

Jane: Oh dear...well I suppose it's better than having ***a***_____***beak*** like Mrs. Jones living next

        door.

Bob: Mrs. Jones?

Jane: Yes... you know ***the busy***_____ from number five. She knows everything that's

        going_____ in the street..... In fact she's probably watching us right now.

Bob: Yeah, probably.

Jane: Oh well. It takes all kinds to make a world.

> **Now check your answers by comparing this page with CONVERSATION 1**

In order to become more familiar with these new everyday expressions,

1) **Listen to Conversation 1 again and tick the boxes** ☐ **next to the expressions as you hear them.**

2) **After the conversation has finished, write in the definitions you can remember. (Some have been done for you as examples.)**

3) **Check your answers by turning to page 92.**

☐ out of sorts...

☐ not sleep a wink..

☐ a racket..

☐ all hours...

☐ couldn't care less..

☐ fed up..

☐ go crook on..

☐ make waves..

☐ stroppy.. *angry / difficult to deal with*...........................

☐ aggro...

☐ way out..

☐ an eyesore..

☐ terrific..

☐ spot on...

☐ easy to get on with......................*friendly*...

☐ hassles...

☐ standoffish...

☐ give (someone) the cold shoulder..

☐ be stuck up............................. *...snobbish / to think you are superior to other people*......

☐ a stickybeak...

☐ a busybody...

☐ going on..............................*happening*...

LANGUAGE NOTE:

In this unit, the Australian expression, *a stickybeak* means a person who always wants to know what other people are doing. However in Unit 4, "Talking about Shopping'" to *"__have a stickybeak__"* (or *a sticky*) means to have a look at something.

LANGUAGE REVIEW

Complete the sentences, choosing from the everyday expressions which are listed in the box below. You can use the clues in brackets ( ) at the end of each sentence to help you. Then complete the crossword using the everyday expressions you have written. The first one has been done as an example.

eyesore	stickybeaks	~~standoffish~~	all hours	terrific
stuck up	make waves	go crook	cold shoulder	aggro.

ACROSS

1) My boyfriend's parents aren't very friendly to me. They are ***standoffish*** towards me when I visit them. (unfriendly)

3) I wish the people next door would tidy their garden. It's an _____. (unpleasant place to look at)

5) Some people get _____ when they drink too much alcohol. (aggressive)

7) Last night, I stayed up till ___ _____ ,finishing my homework. (very late at night)

9) Your idea sounds _____. It's a wonderful suggestion! (excellent)

DOWN

2) My in-laws are very _____ __ . They think they are superior to me. (snobbish)

4) My neighbour's car is very noisy but I don't want to _____ _____ so I won't say anything to them about it. (cause trouble)

6) My neighbour gives me the ____ _____ every time I try to say hello. She doesn't want to be friendly. (deliberately ignores)

8) My neighbours made a racket last night because they had a party. I won't ___ _____ on them because they are usually very quiet. (tell them I'm displeased)

10) The people who live across the road are _____. They are always watching what we are doing. (people who want to know what other people are doing)

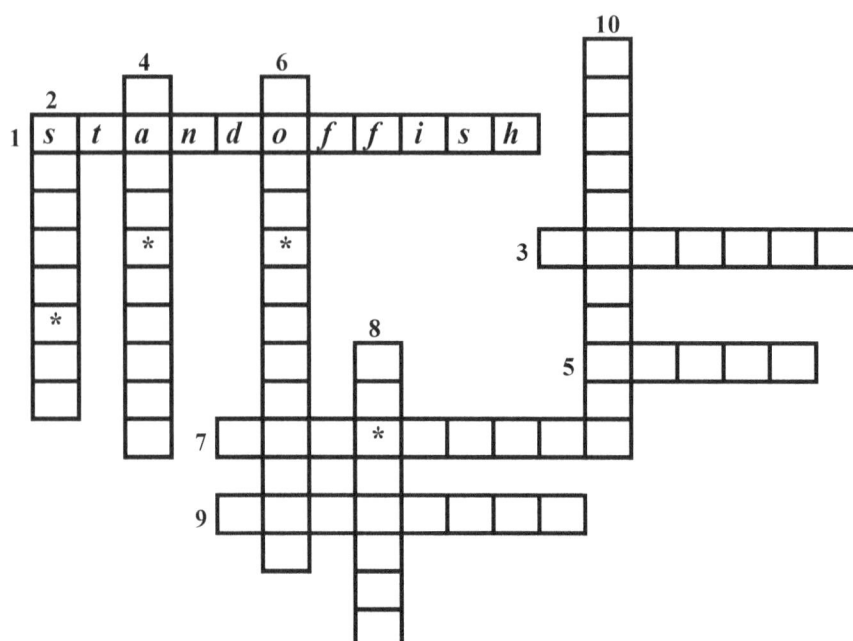

(Answers: page 84)

FOCUS ON SPOKEN LANGUAGE

CHANGING THE TOPIC DURING A CONVERSATION

In spoken English we use certain expressions when we want to change the topic of conversation or when something that is said reminds us of something else we want to ask or talk about. Some of these expressions are:

By the way,.....
eg. "It's very cold outside today, isn't it. *By the way*, I've ordered a new heater for the office. It was a very good price."

While I think of it,..........
eg. "It's very cold outside today, isn't it. *While I think of it*, I've ordered a new heater for the office. It was a very good price."

That reminds me,.........
eg. "It's very cold outside today, isn't it. *That reminds me*, I've ordered a new heater for the office. It was a very good price."

Listen to Conversation 1 again. You will notice that Jane changes the topic of conversation from complaining about her neighbours to asking about Bob's new neighbours. Which expression does she use to introduce the new topic. Write the expression in the space below.

_____(Answer: page 84)

Each of these expressions serve a similar purpose, i.e. to introduce a different topic or new thought to a conversation. However, there are slight differences in their meaning and usage. *"While I think of it...."* and *"That reminds me.........."* are often used when the speaker remembers something that they want to tell or ask the person they are talking to, but *"By the way....."* has more general usage. In order to become more familiar with their usage, listen to everyday conversations as often as you can.

GIVING AN OPINION

In spoken English, we show that we are giving or expressing our opinion in several ways. We can introduce our opinion by saying, *"In my opinion,* the price of petrol is unfair."
or "The price of petrol is unfair, *in my opinion."*

Another way to introduce our opinion is: *"If you ask me,* the price of petrol is unfair."
or "The price of petrol is unfair, *if you ask me."*

Which of these expressions did Bob use when he was talking about his neighbours? Check Conversation 1 and write your answer below.

_____(Answer: page 84)
Give your opinion of this book, using one or more of the above expressions.

_____

(Units 1 - 3)

This section reviews some of the expressions that were introduced in Units 1, 2, and 3 and gives you a chance to see what you have remembered.

- Look at the pictures on the opposite page and decide what the people are saying by choosing from the expressions below.

- Match each picture with an appropriate expression by writing the correct letter in the box next to each expression.

- For extra practice, you could write the appropriate expression in the space provided in the picture.

(Answers: page 84)

1) This is beyond me. I don't understand a word of this. ☐

2) Unfortunately poor eyesight runs in our family. ☐

3) It looks like we'll have to start from scratch, my dear. ☐

4) I can't understand why she is so stuck up. ☐

5) Your work is spot on. I'm very happy with it. ☐

6) Look at Mrs Jones. She's such a stickybeak! ☐

7) I've got the hang of this at last! ☐

8) Keep in touch, won't you? ☐

9) Well, it looks like we're all in the same boat! ☐

UNIT 4

TALKING ABOUT SHOPPING

Some people love shopping while others hate it. A person who loves shopping is sometimes jokingly called a "shopaholic". This means shopping has become a habit that they can't stop. Do you know any shopaholics?

Listen to this conversation between friends who are shopping. (Unit 4 on your audio recording.) The conversation contains many colloquial or everyday expressions which will be explained later in the unit - so don't worry if you don't understand every word. This time you are only listening for gist or general understanding of the topic. As you listen, tick the correct answers below. (There may be more than one correct answer.)

When you have finished you can check your answers on page 84.

1) What does Mari (first speaker) want to shop around for?

        a) a book

        b) a pair of shoes

        c) some furniture

2) Ingrid and Mari are having the conversation:

        a) before they start shopping.

        b) after they have finished shopping.

3) Ingrid and Mari

        a) both enjoy shopping.

        b) both hate shopping.

4) What time are the friends going to meet again?

        a) twelve o' clock

        b) two o' clock

        c) two thirty.

Now we'll look at the everyday expressions used in the conversation - turn to the next page.

CONVERSATION 1 (with everyday expressions)

Read this conversation as you listen to the audio recording. Do you know what the _underlined_ words mean? They are colloquial or everyday expressions.

Mari: I'm _**a bit broke**_ at the moment Ingrid, so I can't spend much today but I'd like to _**shop around**_ for a pair of shoes that don't _**cost an arm and a leg**_.

Ingrid: Yeah, some shoes are _**a rip-off**_ aren't they? We could _**check out**_ the new shoe-shop next to the _**deli**_.

Mari: Maybe - I think that shop looks a bit _**pricey**_ but we can have a look. I want to _**pick up**_ a few _**bits and pieces**_ at the deli anyway. _**What're you after?**_

Ingrid: Well I need to get a few _**vegies**_, then I'm going to have _**a spending spree!**_ I want to buy some _**going out gear**_, some new _**undies**_ for the kids, a new _**nightie**_ and a new _**cozzie**_ for me ....and of course I'll have a look for some _**Chrissie**_ presents.....

Mari: Hold on a minute Ingrid! I'd love to help you look for all those things but I'm a bit _**pushed for**_ time today. Look why don't we _**split up**_ and meet back in a couple of hours for a quick _**cuppa**_ and then I can have _**a stickybeak**_ at what you've bought.

Ingrid: OK, if you like.

Mari: By the way, you should check out the dress shop next to the chemist for your going out gear. They had some nice things there last week.

Ingrid: OK, that sounds like a good idea. See you back here at two o' clock then.

Mari: OK, you won't _**get carried away**_ with your shopping and _**lose track of**_ time though, will you? I'll have to go at two thirty.

Ingrid: Don't worry, I won't! See you then.

Now let's see what these expressions mean - look at the next page.

CONVERSATION 2 (explanation of everyday expressions)

Compare Conversation 1 with Conversation 2 - You will see that some of the words
are different but the meaning is the same in both conversations. Find the underlined words
in Conversation 1, then underline the words with the same meaning in Conversation 2.
For example: <u>a bit broke</u> (Conversation 1) = <u>don't have much money</u> (Conversation 2)

Mari: I <u>don't have much money</u> at the moment Ingrid, so I can't spend much today but I'd like
to visit a few shops to look for the best price for a pair of shoes that don't cost too much
money.

Ingrid: Yeah, some shoes are over-priced aren't they? We could look at the new shoe-shop
next to the delicatessen (the shop which sells cooked meat and cheese.)

Mari: Maybe - I think that shop looks a bit expensive but we can have a look. I want to get
a few small items at the deli anyway. What're you looking for?

Ingrid: Well I need to get some vegetables, then I'm going to have an enjoyable time spending
money. I want to buy some clothes for parties, some new underwear for the kids, a
new night dress to wear to bed and a new swimming costume for me ....and of course
I'll have a look for some Christmas presents.....

Mari: Hold on a minute Ingrid! I'd love to help you look for all those things but I don't have
enough time today. Look why don't we go separately (not together) and meet back in a
couple of hours for a quick cup of tea or coffee and then I can have a look at what
you've bought.

Ingrid: OK, if you like.

Mari :   By the way, you should check out the dress shop next to the chemist for your going out
clothes. They had some nice things there last week.

Ingrid: OK, that sounds like a good idea. See you back here at two o'clock then.

Mari: OK, you won't become too interested and involved with your shopping and forget
about time though, will you? I'll have to go at two thirty.

Ingrid: Don't worry, I won't! See you then.

> **Now to become familiar with the everyday expressions,**
> **practise reading CONVERSATION 1 aloud with a partner.**

Listen to the conversation again and fill in the missing words. You may need to listen more than once. (Don't worry about your spelling as this activity focuses on listening skills; you can check your spelling later.)

Mari: I'm _a bit_____ at the moment Ingrid, so I can't spend much today but I'd like to _shop_

          around for a pair of shoes that don't _cost an arm and a_____.

Ingrid: Yeah, some shoes are _a_____ aren't they? We could _check_____ the new shoe-

          shop next to the _deli_.

Mari: Maybe - I think that shop looks a bit _pricey_ but we can have a look. I want to _pick up_

          a few _____ _and pieces_ at the deli anyway. _What're you_____?

Ingrid: Well I need to get a few _vegies,_ then I'm going to have _a spending spree!_ I want to buy

          some _going out_____, some new _____ for the kids, a new _nightie_ and a new

          _____ for me ....and of course I'll have a look for some _Chrissie_ presents.....

Mari: Hold on a minute Ingrid! I'd love to help you look for all those things but I'm a bit

          _____ _for_ time today. Look why don't we _split_____ and meet back in a couple of

          hours for a quick _____ and then I can have _a_____ _beak_ at what you've bought.

Ingrid: OK, if you like.

Mari: By the way, you should check out the dress shop next to the chemist for your going out

          gear. They had some nice things there last week.

Ingrid: OK, that sounds like a good idea. See you back here at two o 'clock then.

Mari: OK, you won't _get_____ _away_ with your shopping and _lose_____ _of_ time though,

          will you? I'll have to go at two thirty.

Ingrid: Don't worry, I won't! See you then.

> **Now check your answers by comparing this page with CONVERSATION 1**

In order to become more familiar with these new everyday expressions,

1) **Listen to Conversation 1 again and tick the boxes ☐ next to the expressions as you hear them.**
2) **After the conversation has finished, write in the definitions you can remember. (Some have been done for you as examples.)**
3) **Check your answers by turning to page 93.**

☐ to be a bit broke.............................*to not have much money*...

☐ shop around..

☐ cost an arm and a leg..

☐ a rip-off...

☐ to check out...

☐ a deli.....................................*delicatessen (a shop which sells cooked meat and cheese)*

☐ pricey..

☐ pick up...

☐ bits and pieces...

☐ What are you after?...

☐ vegies..

☐ a spending spree.........................*an enjoyable time spending money*.................................

☐ going out gear...

☐ undies..

☐ nightie...

☐ cozzie..

☐ Chrissie...

☐ (to be) pushed for.........................*to not have enough*..

☐ split up..

☐ cuppa..

☐ have a stickybeak..

☐ get carried away..

☐ lose track of..............................*forget about*...

LANGUAGE NOTE:

In Unit 3 "Talking about the Neighbours", the expression "*stickybeak*" meant a person who always wants to know what other people are doing.

In this unit, "Talking about Shopping" to "*have a stickybeak*" (or *a sticky*) means to have a look at something.

LANGUAGE REVIEW

Complete the sentences, choosing from the everyday expressions which are listed below. You can use the clues in brackets ( ) at the end of each sentence to help you. Then complete the crossword using the everyday expressions you have written. The first one has been done as an example.

lose track	broke	stickybeak	vegies	check out	pricey	Chrissie
cozzie	pushed	deli	spending spree	cuppa	rip off	

ACROSS

1) Let's stop and have a ***cuppa***. I'm thirsty! (cup of tea or coffee)
3) It's easy to _____ _____ of time when you are having fun. (forget about)
5) Are you going to open your presents now so that I can have a _____. (look)
7) What kind of _____ would you like with dinner tonight? (vegetables)
9) Could you go to the _____ for me and buy some cheese? (shop which sells cooked meat and cheese)
11) I'd love to buy this car but it's too _____. (expensive)
13) Have you done your _____ shopping yet? (Christmas)

DOWN

2) I'm _____ for time today so I'll have to hurry. (don't have enough)
4) I had a _____ _____ with my credit card but now I have to pay for it. (an enjoyable time spending money)
6) Today we visited lots of real estate agents to _____ _____ the prices of houses. (look at)
8) I'm _____ all the time. I don't know where all my money goes! (don't have money)
10) Bring your _____ with you when you come to our house. We have a swimming pool at our place. (swimming costume)
12) Look at the price of this car! It's a _____ ____! (overpriced)

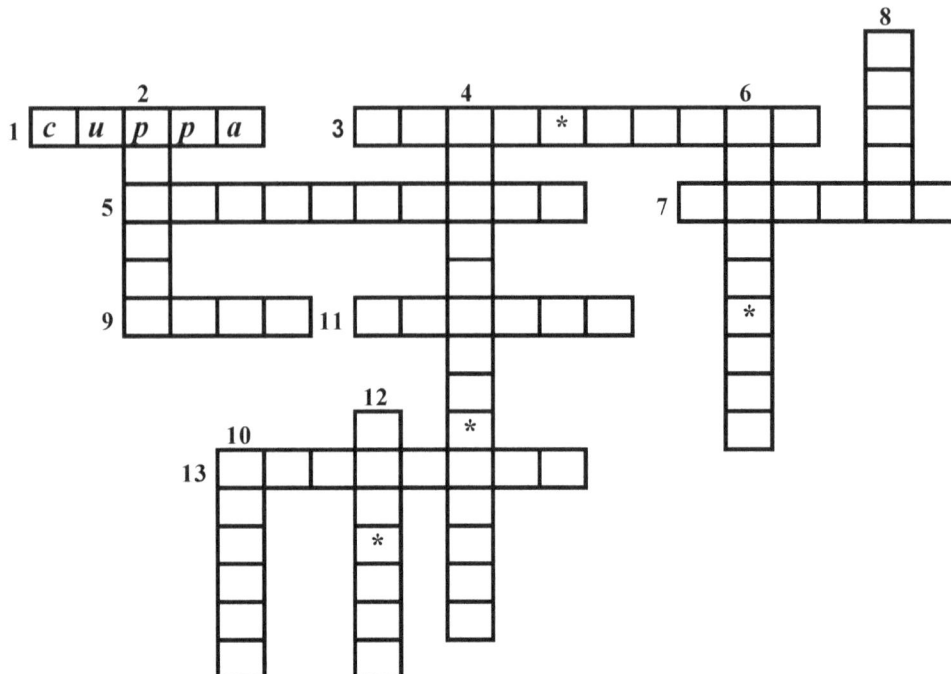

(Answers: page 85)

FOCUS ON SPOKEN LANGUAGE - REVISION

In Part 6 (*Focus on Spoken Language*) of Units 1, 2 and 3 we have looked at different conversation strategies of spoken English. In Unit 1, we looked at the use of *contractions*. (e.g. I'll, we're, won't.) In Unit 2, we looked at the use of *question tags*. (e.g. "She'll like that, won't she?") In Unit 3, we looked at the use of *"By the way...."* to change to a new topic during a conversation.

In this section, we will revise the above conversation strategies. Look at Conversation 1 of this unit again (page 29). Each of the above conversation strategies have been used by Mari or Ingrid during Conversation 1, "*Talking about Shopping*".

REVISION EXERCISES

A) Find and circle the contractions that have been used in Conversation 1.

B) Find the sentences with question tags. (There are two sentences) Write them below under the correct section. (There is no reply to the first sentence.)

Remember the pattern!

If the first part of the sentence has a *positive* verb, the question tag is *negative*.
If the first part of the sentence has a *negative* verb, the question tag is *positive.*
When the speaker is using a question tag to be conversational, the reply usually agrees with the statement in the first part of the sentence.

Statement	**Question tag**	**Short reply**
1)		(No Reply)
2)		

C) In Conversation 1, Mari suggests to Ingrid that they should *split up* and meet back later for a *cuppa* and *a stickybeak* at what she has bought. Then she changes the topic of conversation. Listen to the conversation again. What does she change the topic of the conversation to? What expression does she use to introduce the new topic? Write the sentence she uses below.

_____

_____(Answers page 85)

LANGUAGE NOTE:
Look at Conversation 1 again and notice Ingrid's reply when Mari suggested that they should split up and meet in a couple of hours for a cuppa. She said, "OK. If you like." The expression, "If you like." is a conversational expression which means "I agree with your suggestion/plan, if that is what you want to do."

UNIT 5

VISITING THE DOCTOR

"We'll run a few tests and see what we come up with."

Unit 5 - VISITING THE DOCTOR - Part 1

Before you listen to the conversation between a doctor and patient (Unit 5 on your audio recording), check the meaning of the following words in a dictionary if you are not familiar with their meaning.

| prescription | examination | symptoms | diarrhoea |

Write the word next to its correct meaning below: (Answers: page 85.)

- a sickness which causes frequent visits to the toilet_____

- signs or changes to the health of a person_____

- a doctor's written instruction for the use of medicine_____

- a careful inspection_____

Listen to the conversation between a doctor and patient. The conversation contains many colloquial or everyday expressions which will be explained later in the unit - so don't worry if you don't understand every word. This time you are only listening for gist or general understanding of the topic. As you listen, tick the correct answer below. There may be more than one correct answer. Answers: page 85.

1) Mrs Smith is visiting the doctor because:

      a) her daughter is sick.

      b) she is pregnant.

      c) her son is sick.

      d) she feels unwell.

2) One of Mrs Smith's symptoms is:

      a) a backache.

      b) a headache.

      c) vomiting.

3) The doctor suggests that she should:

      a) have an operation.

      b) have a few days off work.

      c) take some headache tablets.

> **Now we'll look at the everyday expressions used in the conversation - turn to the next page.**

CONVERSATION 1 (with everyday expressions)

Read this conversation as you listen to the audio tape. Do you know what the _underlined_ words mean? They are colloquial or 'everyday' expressions.

Doctor: What seems to be the problem, Mrs Smith?

Mrs. Smith: Well actually, it's my son. He's been **_off colour_** since yesterday.
At first I thought he was **_putting it on_** because he didn't want to go to school but then he started **_throwing up_** and he's had **_the runs_** as well. He's **_picked up_** a lot today but he still seems to be a bit **_washed out_**.

Doctor: Mm. He's probably got the **_bug_** that's going around. **_Pop_** him on the table and I'll give him a **_check up_**. Has he complained about a sore **_tummy?_**

Mrs. Smith: He did yesterday - not so much today.

Doctor: Mm. Just **_keep an eye on_** him. I'll give you a prescription for some medicine but I think he's **_on the mend._** Is there anything else?

Mrs. Smith: Yes. Could you **_take a look at_** me while I'm here? I think I'm **_coming down with something._** Usually I'm **_as fit as a fiddle_** but the last couple of days I've been feeling really **_crook._**

Doctor: Mm. It could be the same **_bug_**.... Any other symptoms?

Mrs. Smith: Yes. I feel really **_washed out_** and I've had **_a splitting headache._**

Doctor: And when did these symptoms **_come on?_**

Mrs. Smith: About five days ago.... but I've been having bad headaches for a while now.

Doctor: Mm. Have you been **_overdoing it_** lately? Are you worrying about something?

Mrs. Smith: I suppose I am **_a worrywart_** and I've been **_pretty uptight_** lately about work at the office.

Doctor: Well, first of all, I think you need a few days off work to **_take it easy._** If the problem doesn't **_clear up_** in a few days we'll run some tests and see what we **_come up with._**

Mrs. Smith: OK. Thankyou Doctor.

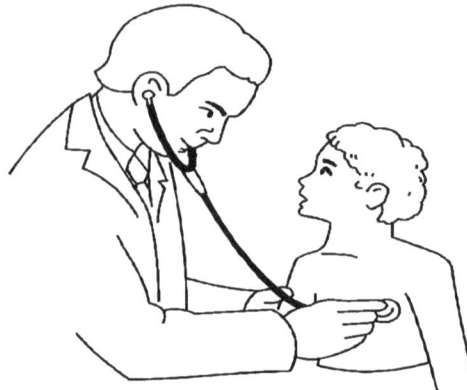

Now let's see what these expressions mean - look at the next page.

CONVERSATION 2 (explanation of everyday expressions)

Compare Conversation 1 with Conversation 2 -You will see that some of the words are different but the meaning is the same in both conversations. Find the underlined words in Conversation 1, then underline the words with the same meaning in Conversation 2. For example: <u>off colour</u> (Conversation 1) = <u>sick</u> (Conversation 2)

Doctor:	What seems to be the problem, Mrs Smith?
Mrs. Smith:	Well actually, it's my son. He's been <u>sick</u> since yesterday. At first I thought he was pretending because he didn't want to go to school but then he started vomiting and he's had diarrhoea as well. He's improved a lot today but he still seems to be a bit unwell/tired.
Doctor:	Mm. He's probably got the virus that's going around. Put him on the table and I'll give him an examination. Has he complained about a sore stomach?
Mrs. Smith:	He did yesterday - not so much today.
Doctor:	Mm. Just keep a careful watch on him. I'll give you a prescription for some medicine but I think he's improving (in health). Is there anything else?
Mrs. Smith:	Yes. Could you examine me while I'm here. I think I'm getting a sickness. Usually I'm very healthy but the last couple of days I've been feeling really unwell/sick.
Doctor:	Mm. It could be the same virus.... Any other symptoms?
Mrs. Smith:	Yes. I feel really unwell/tired and I've had a very bad headache.
Doctor:	And when did these symptoms begin?
Mrs. Smith:	About five days ago.... but I've been having bad headaches for a while now.
Doctor:	Mm. Have you been working too hard lately? Are you worrying about something?
Smith:	I suppose I am a person who worries too much and I've been quite anxious lately about work at the office.
Doctor:	Well, first of all, I think you need a few days off work to relax. If the problem doesn't become better in a few days we'll run some tests and see what we find.
Mrs. Smith:	OK. Thankyou Doctor.

Now to become familiar with the everyday expressions, practise reading CONVERSATION 1 aloud with a partner.

Listen to the conversation again and fill in the missing words. You may have to listen more than once. Don't worry about your spelling as this exercise focuses on listening skills - you can check your spelling later.

Doctor: What seems to be the problem, Mrs Smith?

Mrs. Smith: Well actually, it's my son. He's been *off*_____ since yesterday.

At first I thought he was *putting it on* because he didn't want to go to

school but then he started *throwing*_____ and he's had *the*_____ as well.

He's *picked*_____ a lot today but he still seems to be a bit *washed*_____.

Doctor: Mm. He's probably got the _____ that's going around. *Pop* him on the table and

I'll give him a *check*_____. Has he complained about a sore _____?

Mrs. Smith: He did yesterday - not so much today.

Doctor: Mm. Just *keep an*_____ *on* him. I'll give you a prescription for some

medicine but I think he's *on the*_____. Is there anything else?

Mrs. Smith: Yes. Could you *take a*_____ *at* me while I'm here. I think I'm *coming*

_____ *with something*. Usually I'm *as*_____ *as a fiddle* but the last couple

of days I've been feeling really _____.

Doctor: Mm. It could be the same *bug*... Any other symptoms?

Mrs. Smith: Yes. I feel really *washed out* and I've had *a*_____ *headache*.

Doctor: And when did these symptoms *come*_____?

Mrs. Smith: About five days ago.... but I've been having bad headaches

for a while now.

Doctor: Mm. Have you been _____ *doing it* lately? Are you worrying

about something?

Mrs. Smith: I suppose I am *a worrywart* and I've been *pretty*_____ *tight* lately about

work at the office.

Doctor: Well first of all, I think you need a few days off work to

*take it*_____. If the problem doesn't *clear up* in a few days we'll run

some tests and see what we *come*_____ *with* .

Mrs. Smith: OK. Thankyou Doctor.

Now check your answers by comparing this page with
CONVERSATION 1

In order to become more familiar with these new everyday expressions,

1) **Listen to Conversation 1 again and tick the boxes** ☐ **next to the expressions as you hear them.**

2) **After the conversation has finished, write in the definitions you can remember. (Some have been done for you as examples.)**

3) **Check your answers by turning to page 94.**

☐ off colour...

☐ putting it on.................................*pretending / acting*...................................

☐ to throw up...

☐ the runs............................. *diarrhoea (causes frequent visits to the toilet)*........

☐ pick up...

☐ washed out...

☐ a/the bug...

☐ pop...

☐ a check up...

☐ tummy...

☐ keep an eye on...

☐ on the mend..

☐ take a look at...

☐ coming down with (something)..

☐ fit as a fiddle..................................... *very healthy*.......................................

☐ to feel crook..

☐ a splitting headache...

☐ come on..

☐ overdoing it ....

☐ a worrywart..................................... *a person who worries too much*..............

☐ pretty uptight..

☐ take it easy..

☐ clear up...

☐ come up with...

LANGUAGE NOTE:
In Unit 3, the expression **" go crook on"** was used to mean "tell someone you are displeased or angry". However, when talking about health, to **"be crook"** means to be unwell.

LANGUAGE REVIEW

Complete the sentences, using the everyday expressions which have been listed below. You can use the clues in brackets ( ) at the end of each sentence to help you. Then complete the crossword using the everyday expressions you have written. The first one has been done as an example. Answers page 85.

off colour	throw up	on the mend	come down with	fit as a fiddle	keep an eye on
come up with	take it easy	the runs	~~putting it on~~	washed out	pick up	crook

ACROSS

1. She's not really sick, she's ***putting it on.*** (pretending)
3. I feel _____ _____ today. (sick / unwell)
5. I need to go to the toilet quickly. I've got _____ _____. (diarrhoea)
7. He feels sick today but I'm sure he will _____ ____ by tomorrow. (improve in health)
9. If he tries very hard, he will _____ ____ _____ the answer. (find)
11. The doctor told me to _____ ___ _____.(rest, relax)
13. I'm not going to work today, I feel _____. (sick)

DOWN

2. Everyone has the flu. I hope I don't _____ _____ _____ it.(get sick)
4. I feel sick in the stomach. I think I'm going to _____ ____. (vomit)
6. I was crook yesterday but I'm ____ ____ _____ now. (improving in health)
8. He doesn't look well. He looks _____ _____. (tired)
10. He never gets sick. He's as _____ ___ ___ _____. (very healthy)
12. _____ ___ _____ ____ the baby please. (watch carefully)

FOCUS ON SPOKEN LANGUAGE - STAGES IN A MEDICAL CONSULTATION

When we visit a doctor, he or she usually has to ask a lot of questions about symptoms to decide what the problem may be. This is called a medical consultation. There are usually certain steps or stages in a consultation with a doctor after the initial greeting. For example:

1) **The doctor asks about the problem.**
2) **The patient talks about the symptoms (and answers the doctor's questions.)**
3) **The doctor examines the patient (and asks further questions.)**
4) **The doctor suggests what he/she thinks the problem may be.**
5) **The doctor suggests some treatment or further tests.**
6) **Closing of consultation.**

Of course, **not all** consultations are **exactly** the same. Sometimes the doctor suggests what the problem might be **before** he/she examines the patient (or he/she may not need to examine the patient.) Look at Conversation 1 again (below) and write the number of the stage next to each section of the consultation. In this consultation, the doctor has **two** patients, Mrs Smith and her son, so some stages will occur more than once. Some sections have been numbered for you. (Answers page 86.)

Doctor:	What seems to be the problem, Mrs Smith?	
Mrs. Smith:	Well actually, it's my son. He's been **off colour** since yesterday. At first I thought he was **putting it on** because he didn't want to go to school but then he started **throwing up** and he's had **the runs** as well. He's **picked up** a lot today but he still seems to be a bit **washed out.**	
Doctor:	Mm. He's probably got the **bug** that's going around.	
	Pop him on the table and I'll give him a **check up.** Has he complained about a sore **tummy?**	
Mrs. Smith:	He did yesterday - not so much today.	
Doctor:	Mm. Just **keep an eye on** him. I'll give you a prescription for some medicine but I think he's **on the mend.**	
	Is there anything else?	**1**
Mrs. Smith:	Yes. Could you **take a look at** me while I'm here? I think I'm coming **down with something.** Usually I'm **as fit as a fiddle** but the last couple of days I've been feeling really **crook.**	
Doctor:	Mm. It could be the same bug....	**4**
	Any other symptoms?	
Mrs. Smith:	Yes. I feel really **washed out** and I've had **a splitting headache.**	
Doctor:	And when did these symptoms **come on?**	
Mrs. Smith:	About five days ago.... but I've been having bad headaches for a while now.	**2**
Doctor:	Mm. Have you been **overdoing it** lately? Are you worrying about something?	
Mrs. Smith:	I suppose I am **a worrywart** and I've been **pretty uptight** lately about work at the office.	
Doctor	Well, first of all, I think you need a few days off work to **take it easy.** If the problem doesn't **clear up** in a few days we'll run some tests and see what we **come up with.**	
Mrs. Smith:	OK. Thankyou Doctor.	

UNIT 6

WORRYING ABOUT MONEY

"How are we going to make ends meet this month ?"

There's an expression in English that says, "Money doesn't go very far."
What do you think it means? In English we also say. "Money doesn't grow on trees!"
Do you have similar expressions about money in your first language?

In modern society, it is becoming a common practice for people to use "plastic money" or credit cards to pay for the things they need or want. Do you think credit cards are a good idea?

Listen to this conversation about money. (Unit 6 on your audio recording.) The conversation contains many colloquial or everyday expressions which will be explained later in the unit - so don't worry if you don't understand every word. This time you are only listening for general understanding of the topic. As you listen, tick the correct answers below. (There may be more than one correct answer.) When you have finished you can check you answers on page 86.

1) Where is the conversation taking place?

    a) at work

    b) at home

    c) at the bank

2) What is the topic of conversation?

    a) household bills

    b) bank charges

    c) a tax form

3) During the conversation the speakers

    a) have different opinions

    b) have similar opinions

Now we'll look at the everyday expressions used in the conversation - turn to the next page.

CONVERSATION 1 (with everyday expressions)

Read this conversation as you listen to the audio tape. Do you know what the _underlined_ words mean? They are colloquial or everyday expressions.

Husband: _Good grief_! Look at this phone bill! It's _gone through the roof_ this time.

Wife: Oh no, really. What're _we up for_ this time?

Husband: $305... Oh, I don't know. We just don't seem to be able to _get ahead_.

Wife: Mm. I know what you mean. I can't _figure out_ where all the money goes. We always seem to be _forking out_ for one bill or another. Maybe we'd better sit down and _work out_ a budget.

Husband: Yeah OK. _It's got me beat_ though. Jim at work earns the same as me yet they seem to be pretty _well off_. They _splurged_ on an expensive holiday last month, and here we are, we _can't make ends meet._

Wife   Yes, but maybe they used plastic money.

Husband: Mm maybe, _who knows_. I'd be happy if we could just _get by_ and have a bit spare to _put away_ each week to build _a nest egg_ - you know, _something to fall back on_ if something unexpected happens.

Wife: I know what you mean. I'm sick of _being flat broke_ all the time too. We'll have to talk to the kids about _going easy on_ their phone calls in future.

Husband: Well, better still, we could ask them to _chip in_ for the phone bill seeing they're the ones who are on the phone for hours, _chatting_ to their friends. And they've both got part-time jobs now.

Wife: Mm that sounds fair enough to me. We could talk to them about it tonight.

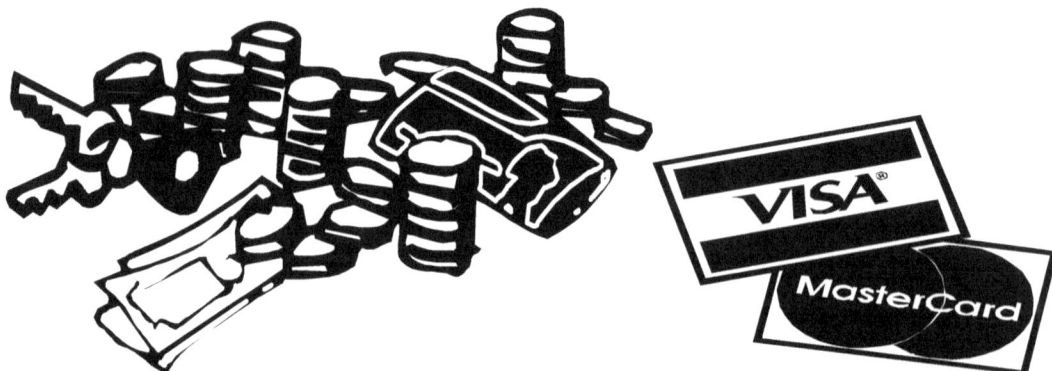

Now let's see what these expressions mean - look at the next page.

CONVERSATION 2 (explanation of everyday expressions)

Compare Conversation 1 with Conversation 2 -**You will see that some of the words are different but the meaning is the same in both conversations. Find the underlined words in Conversation 1, then underline the words with the same meaning in Conversation 2. For example:** <u>Good grief!</u> **(Conversation 1) =** <u>This is a shock!</u>**(Conversation 2)**

Husband: <u>This is a shock!</u> Look at this phone bill! It's reached an extreme price this time.

Wife: Oh no really? What do we have to pay this time?

Husband: $305... Oh I don't know. We just don't seem to be able to progress financially.

Wife: Mm. I know what you mean. I can't understand where all the money goes. We always seem to be unwillingly/reluctantly paying for one bill or another. Maybe we'd better sit down and plan the details of a budget.

Husband: Yes OK. I don't understand though. Jim at work earns the same as me, yet they seem to be pretty wealthy. They spent a lot of money on an expensive holiday last month, and here we are, we aren't able to pay our expenses.

Wife   Yes, but maybe they used plastic money.

Husband: Mm maybe, I don't know the answer to that. I'd be happy if we could just manage our situation without difficulty and have a bit spare to save each week to build up some savings for the future - you know a reserve for future use if something unexpected happens.

Wife: Mm I know what you mean. I'm sick of having no money all the time too. We'll have to talk to the children about using less/spending less (time) on their phone calls in future.

Husband: Well, better still, we could ask them to contribute some money for the phone bill seeing they're the ones who are on the phone for hours, talking informally to their friends. And they've both got part-time jobs now.

Wife: Mm that sounds fair enough to me. We could talk to them about it tonight.

> **Now to become familiar with the everyday expressions, practise reading CONVERSATION 1 aloud with a partner.**

Listen to the conversation again and fill in the missing words. You may have to listen more than once. (Don't worry about your spelling as this exercise focuses on listening skills - you can check your spelling later.)

Husband: ___Good grief___! Look at this phone bill! It's ___gone through the___ _____ this time.

Wife: Oh no, really. What're ___we___ _____ ___for___ this time?

Husband: $305... Oh I don't know. We just don't seem to be able to ___get ahead___.

Wife: Mm. I know what you mean. I can't ___figure___ _____ where all the money goes. We always seem to be ___forking___ _____ for one bill or another. Maybe we'd better sit down and _____ ___out___ a budget.

Husband: Yeah OK. ___It's got me___ _____ though. Jim at work earns the same as me - yet they seem to be pretty _____ ___off___. They ___splurged___ on an expensive holiday last month, and here we are, we ___can't___ _____ ___ends___ _____.

Wife Yeah but maybe they used plastic money.

Husband: Mm maybe, ___who___ _____. I'd be happy if we could just ___get___ ____ and have a bit spare to ___put away___ each week to build up ___a nest___ _____ - you know, ___something to fall___ _____ ___on___ if something unexpected happens.

Wife: I know what you mean. I'm sick of ___being flat___ _____ all the time too. We'll have to talk to the kids about ___going___ _____ ___on___ their phone calls in future.

Husband: Well, better still, we could ask them to _____ ___in___ for the phone bill seeing they're the ones who are on the phone for hours, ___chatting___ to their friends. And they've both got part-time jobs now.

Wife: Mm that sounds fair enough to me. We could talk to them about it tonight.

> **Now check your answers by comparing this page with**
> **CONVERSATION 1**

In order to become more familiar with these new everyday expressions,

1) Listen to Conversation 1 again and tick the boxes ☐ next to the expressions as you hear them.

2) After the conversation has finished, write in the definitions you can remember. (Some have been done for you as examples.)

3) Check your answers by turning to page 95.

☐ Good grief ....*This a shock!*...

☐ Go through the roof...

☐ to be up for ($$$) ....*to have to pay*...

☐ to get ahead ....

☐ figure out ....

☐ forking out ....*unwillingly/reluctantly pay*ing..........................

☐ work out ....

☐ It's got me beat ....

☐ well off ....

☐ splurge ....

☐ not make ends meet..

☐ who knows...

☐ get by...*to manage (under difficult circumstances)*.................

☐ put away (money)..

☐ a nest egg..

☐ something to fall back on..

☐ to be flat broke...

☐ go easy on (something)................*use less / spend less of (something)*.......................

☐ chip in...

☐ chatting...

LANGUAGE NOTE:

'To go easy on (something)' means to use sparingly, not use too much of (something). For example: "Go easy on the milk, there's not much left." means "Don't use too much milk, there's not much left."

LANGUAGE REVIEW

Complete the sentences, using the everyday expressions in this unit which have been listed below. Then complete the crossword using the words you have written. The first one has been done as an example.

flat broke	forking out	~~roof~~	nest egg	chip in	fall back on
	make ends meet	splurged	well off	put away	

ACROSS

1) If the cost of something has reached an extreme price we could say it has gone through the ***roof***.

3) If someone can't pay for their expenses, we could say they can't _____ _____ _____.

5) If we have something in reserve for future use, we could say we have something to _____ _____ ___.

7) If I spent a lot of money on something, I could say I _____ on it.

9) If I don't have any money, I could say I'm _____ _____.

DOWN

2) If you are reluctantly paying for something, you could say you are _____ _____ for it.

4) If I had some money saved, I could call it my _____ _____.

6) If someone is wealthy, we could say they are _____ ____.

8) If we save a small amount of money each week, we could say we _____ _____ a little money each week.

10) If a group of people are going to contribute money for a friend's wedding present, we say they are going to _____ ____ for the present.

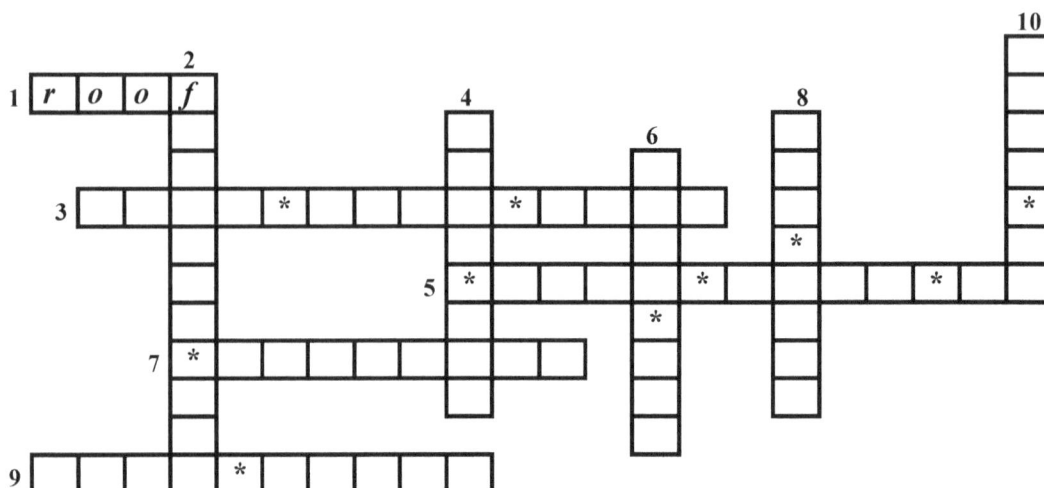

(Answers: page 86)

FOCUS ON SPOKEN LANGUAGE - GIVING FEEDBACK

When having a conversation in English, it is very important to give 'feedback'. This means to show that we are listening and understand what our partner is saying. We do this by using such expressions as 'Yes,...', Mm.......', 'Well.......', 'I know what you mean.....', etc. Listen to Conversation 1 again and notice the expressions used by the speakers to give feedback. The conversation would sound very abrupt and unnatural without such expressions. In some cultures this aspect of communication is not so important but when communicating in English it is necessary to give feedback to your partner if you want to show you are interested and understand what has been said.

We also use non-verbal feedback such as smiling and nodding our head when we agree with what is being said or frowning and shaking our head if we hear bad news, don't understand or disagree with the speaker. Someone who doesn't give feedback or show that they are listening and interested is called 'deadpan', meaning they don't show any reaction or expression on their face. So remember to give feedback!

GIVING REASONS - JUSTIFYING ACTIONS AND OPINIONS

A common word used to introduce a reason for an action or opinion in spoken English is *'because'*. e.g. "They should pay for some of the petrol *because* they use the car a lot." In colloquial speech we sometimes use *'seeing'* as a linking word to justify an action or opinion.

In Conversation 1, the husband suggests that the children should contribute some money towards the phone bill, then he gives a reason for (justifies) his opinion. Listen to Conversation 1 again and notice the way he introduces his reason. Complete the following sentence from the conversation.
"We could ask them to chip in for the phone bill_____

_____ ,chatting to their friends."

Look at Conversation 1 again and find another reason why the husband thinks his kids should *chip in* for the phone bill. Use "seeing" as a linking word to complete the following sentence.
He thinks they should chip in for part of the phone bill _____

_____ (Answer: page 87)

We often use 'seeing' when justifying an action we have done or plan to do.
eg. "We'll finish early today *seeing* you've all worked hard and made good progress."
     or
   "I'm going to buy a new jacket, *seeing* I'm going for a job interview next week."

Think of something that you have done recently or plan to do in the future and write a sentence justifying your action using 'seeing'.

_____

_____

_____

(Units 4 - 6)

This section reviews some of the expressions that were introduced in Units 4, 5, and 6 and gives you a chance to see what you have remembered.

- **Look at the pictures on the opposite page and decide what the people are saying by choosing from the expressions below.**

- **Match each picture with an appropriate expression by writing the correct letter in the box next to each expression.**

- **For extra practice, you could write the appropriate expression in the space provided in the picture.**

(Answers: page 87)

1) Look at these prices! What a rip off!   ☐

2) I think I'll have another cuppa.   ☐

3) I think I'm coming down with something. I feel terrible.   ☐

4) We all chipped in to get this for you.   ☐

5) Go easy on the milk or there won't be any left for me!   ☐

6) You look crook. Do you feel OK?   ☐

7) When did this problem come on?   ☐

8) They look well off, don't they?   ☐

9) Sorry I can't make it. I'm pushed for time today.   ☐

UNIT 7

TALKING ABOUT HOLIDAYS

A   B

Before you listen to the conversation about holidays, look at the illustrations on the previous page. Which of the following words describe each holiday? (Answers page 87)

luxury	resort	remote	camping

Write your answers here: A_____ B_____

Listen to the conversation between John and Susan and tick the correct answers. When you have finished, you can check your answers on page 87.

1) Where is the conversation taking place?

    a) at a doctor's surgery

    b) at work

    c) at home

2) What is the topic of conversation?

    a) last year's holiday

    b) their ideas about future holidays

    c) a party during the holidays

3) How long is John going to take off work to travel?

    a) a week

    b) a year

    c) a month

4) During the conversation, the speakers

    a) have different ideas about holidays

    b) agree completely about holidays

Now we'll look at the everyday expressions used in the conversation - turn to the next page.

CONVERSATION 1 - (with everyday expressions)

Read the conversation as you listen to the audio tape. Do you know what the *underlined* words mean? They are colloquial or everyday expressions.

John: I'm glad it's Friday. Bye Susan, I'll see you on Monday.

Susan: Monday? I'll see you at your ***send-off*** tomorrow night.

John: Send-off? I thought I was going to Peter's house for dinner..... So they're having a send-off for me, are they?

Susan: Oh dear. I think I've ***let the cat out of the bag.*** But nobody told me to keep it ***hush hush.***

John: Don't worry. I won't tell anyone you ***spilled the beans.*** It'll be fun!

Susan: Oh good..... I hear that you are taking a year off work to travel. Where are you planning to go?

John: Well, I want to see as much of the world as possible but I want to get ***off the beaten track*** and away from ***the rat race*** of city life. I plan to visit the ***outback*** of Australia first.

Susan: Well, it sounds like you'll be ***on the go.***

John: Oh yes, and I'll have to ***rough it*** but I'll be ***in my element!*** I love camping and ***going bush!***

Susan: Really?...Well, that's not for me. I'd prefer to ***live it up*** at a resort where I'd be ***waited on hand and foot.*** Somewhere I could ***let my hair down***, party at night and then ***take it easy*** beside the pool during the day.

John: Oh no. . .It would ***drive me up the wall*** to lie around a pool all day. That's ***not my cup of tea*** at all.

Susan: Oh well, ***to each his own***. I'll see you on Saturday anyway. And please don't tell anyone I ***let the cat out of the bag.***

John: Don't worry, I won't.

| Now let's see what these expressions mean - look at the next page. |

CONVERSATION 2 - (Explanation of everyday expressions)

Compare Conversation 1 with Conversation 2. You will see that some of the words are different but the meaning is the same in both conversations. Find the underlined expressions in Conversation 1, then, underline the words with the same meaning in Conversation 2. For example: *send-off* (Conversation 1) = *farewell party* (Conversation 2)

John: I'm glad it's Friday. Bye Susan, I'll see you on Monday.

Susan: Monday? I'll see you at your farewell party tomorrow night.

John: Farewell party? I thought I was going to Peter's house for dinner....So they're having a farewell party for me, are they?

Susan: Oh dear. I think I've revealed a secret. But nobody told me to keep it secret.

John: Don't worry. I won't tell anyone that you revealed the secret. It'll be fun!

Susan: Oh good... I hear that you are taking a year off from work to travel. Where are you planning to go?

John: Well, I want to see as much of the world as possible but I want to get away from the populated areas and away from the constantly busy competition of city life. I plan to visit the remote areas of Australia first.

Susan: Well it sounds like you'll be busy.

John: Oh yes, and I'll have to live without basic comforts but I'll be in my preferred situation! I love camping and living close to nature!

Susan: Really?.... Well, that's not for me. I'd prefer to live in luxury at a resort where I'd have all my needs attended to. Somewhere that I could behave very informally, party at night and then relax beside the pool during the day.

John: Oh no...It would greatly irritate me to lie around a pool all day. That's not something which interests me at all.

Susan: Oh well everyone has their own preference. I'll see you on Saturday anyway. And please don't tell anyone that I revealed the secret.

John: Don't worry. I won't.

> Now to become familiar with the everyday expressions, practise reading CONVERSATION 1 aloud with a partner.

Listen to the conversation again and fill in the missing words. You may have to listen more than once. Don't worry about your spelling as this exercise focuses on listening skills. You can check your spelling later.

John: I'm glad it's Friday. Bye Susan, I'll see you on Monday.

Susan: Monday? I'll see you at your **send-_____** tomorrow night.

John: Send-off? I thought I was going to Peter's house for dinner..... So

they're having a send off for me, are they?

Susan: Oh dear. I think I've **let the _____ out of the _____**. But nobody told me to keep it **hush**

hush.

John: Don't worry. I won't tell anyone you **spilled the _____**. It'll be fun!

Susan: Oh good..... I hear that you are taking a year off work to travel. Where

are you planning to go?

John: Well, I want to see as much of the world as possible but I want to get **_____ the beaten**

track and away from **the _____ race** of city life. I plan to visit the **out _____** of

Australia first.

Susan: Well, it sounds like you'll be **on the _____**.

John: Oh yes, and I'll have to **_____ it** but I'll be **in my element!** I love camping and **going**

_____!

Susan: Really?.....Well, that's not for me. I'd prefer to **live it _____** at a resort where I'd be **waited**

on _____ and _____. Somewhere I could **let my _____ down**, party at night and

then **_____ it easy** beside the pool during the day.

John: Oh no. . .It would **drive me up the _____** to lie around a pool all day. That's **not my**

_____ of _____ at all.

Susan: Oh well, **to each his own**. I'll see you on Saturday anyway. And please don't tell

anyone I **let the _____ out of the _____**.

John: Don't worry, I won't.

> **Now check your answers by comparing this page with CONVERSATION 1**

In order to become familiar with these new everyday expressions,

1) **Listen to Conversation 1 again and tick the boxes ☐ next to the expressions as you hear them.**
2) **After the conversation has finished, write in the definitions you can remember. (Some have been done for you as examples.)**
3) **Check your answers by turning to page 96.**

☐ a send-off.................................*a farewell party*..…….

☐ let the cat out of the bag............*reveal a secret*...

☐ hush hush...…....

☐ spill the beans...…....

☐ off the beaten track...….

☐ the rat race..….

☐. outback..….

☐ on the go..…..

☐ to rough it..……..

☐ in one's element......................*in one's preferred situation*...

☐ go bush..……..

☐ live it up...…....

☐ be waited on hand and foot...

☐ let one's hair down...

☐ take it easy...……..

☐ drive (someone) up the wall..

☐ **not** my cup of tea......................*not something which interests me*.............................……

☐ to each his own..……..

LANGUAGE NOTES:
***Outback** Australia is also known as the 'back blocks' of Australia.
*The expression '**not** my cup of tea' is usually used in the negative to refer to an activity or thing which is **not** liked by the speaker.

REVISION EXERCISES

Complete these sentences by choosing the appropriate expressions from the following list. You can use your reference list (previous page) to help you. (Answers: page 87)

rat race	rough it	cup of tea	spilled the beans	take it easy
in my element	off the beaten track		a send-off	drives me up the wall

1) Do you prefer to have a holiday in the city or do you like to get ____ _____ _____ _____ ? (away from populated areas)

2) They gave me __ _____ ___ when I left my last job because I'd been there for many years. (a farewell party)

3) I'm ___ ___ _____ when I'm at the beach. I love to be near the ocean! (in my preferred situation)

4) I am planning to move to the country to get away from the _____ _____. (constantly busy competition of city life)

5) I'm going to _____ ___ _____ on the weekend. I've had a very busy week. (relax)

6) When we first got married, we had to _____ ___ because we didn't have enough money to buy any furniture. (live without basic comforts)

7) I'm very angry with Tom because he _____ ____ _____ to everyone at the office about our plans. (revealed the secret)

8) My next door neighbour _____ ___ ___ ___ _____ by playing loud music all the time. (irritates me greatly)

9) I don't enjoy spending the whole day shopping. It's not my _____ ___ _____ . (*not something which interests me.*)

WHAT ABOUT YOU?

Which kind of holiday would you prefer? Are you "in your element" when camping like John or do you prefer to "live it up" like Susan? Choose from the expressions below to explain your preference. For example: When I go on holiday, I prefer to

get off the beaten track.
rough it.
get away from the rat race.
go bush.
live it up.
be waited on hand and foot.
take it easy.
let my hair down.

Write about your holiday preference.

_____

_____

FOCUS ON SPOKEN LANGUAGE - INTONATION

When speaking in English, we often use "intonation", or the rise and fall of our voice, to express meaning. For example, when we are confused, surprised or think we have misunderstood something that has been said, we may repeat the word or expression with a rise and fall tone to show we don't understand or need the information repeated.

Read the conversation below as you listen to the first part of *Conversation 1* on your audio recording again. You will notice two examples where the speakers have used this conversation strategy (as shown by the arrows ⌒ ⌃).

John: I'm glad it's Friday. Bye Susan, I'll see you on Monday.

Susan: *Monday?* I'll see you at your send-off tomorrow night..

John: *Send-off?* I thought I was going to Peter's house for dinner..... So

          they're having a send-off for me, are they?

Did you hear the rising and falling intonation pattern? Practise the sentences above using rising and falling intonation for the underlined words.

CONVERSATION FILLERS
In spoken English we often begin a reply or comment with a word such as "Well" or "Oh".
As we saw in Unit 6, one reason for this is to give feedback (show we are listening.)
Read Conversation 1 again and notice how many times these expressions are used.
By using words such as "Well" or "Oh, well" at the beginning of a reply, it also gives
us more time to think and softens our reply if we don't agree with what has been said.
For example, Susan's reply at the end of the conversation: "Oh well, to each his own."

STRESSED WORDS IN SPOKEN ENGLISH

Listen to **Conversation 1** again and notice the words which each speaker *stresses*. (These are the words which are easier to hear as the speakers say them more clearly and loudly). Listen to one sentence at a time and underline the stressed words in the conversation with a different coloured pen, then check your answers on page 87.

You will notice that the stressed words are mainly *content* words; names and things (nouns), actions (verbs), and descriptive words rather than the *structural* words ('the', 'in', 'to', 'and'). For example, in the first sentence, "I'm *glad* it's *Friday*", you will notice that the words, *'glad'* and *'Friday'*, are stressed but the words *I'm* and *it's*, are *un*stressed and not as easy to hear. Sometimes *'question words'*, (who, where, why, when) are stressed, such as in Susan's question: *"Where* are you planning to *go*?" Sometimes negatives (no, not, won't) are stressed because they show opinion or intention, as in John's last comment. "*Don't* worry, I *won't*."

NOTE: This is a difficult exercise, so don't worry if you didn't get it right the first time. The aim of the exercise is to make you more aware of the use of stressed and unstressed words in spoken English. Listening for the stressed words in spoken English may help you understand better what is being said as these words help you to guess what the speaker is saying without hearing *every* word. (You probably use this strategy in your first language without realising that you are not listening to every word.)

UNIT 8

PHONING A TRADESPERSON

If you own or rent a house or unit, at some time you will need to have repairs done. This usually means you will need to phone to make arrangements for a tradesperson to come to your home.

Listen to this conversation in which someone is phoning a tradesperson. The customer is speaking to a receptionist. (Unit 8 on your audio recording.) The conversation contains many colloquial or everyday expressions which will be explained later in the unit - so don't worry if you don't understand every word. This time you are only listening for general understanding of the topic. As you listen, tick the correct answers below.

When you have finished you can check you answers on page 88.

---

1) The customer is phoning

    a) a carpenter

    b) a plumber

    c) an electrician

2) What time can the tradesperson visit?

    a) 9 p.m.

    b) 5 p.m.

    c) 6 p.m.

3) What is the customers name?

    a) Mr. Ford

    b) Mr. Ward

    c) Mrs. Sword

Now we'll look at the everyday expressions used in the conversation - turn to the next page.

CONVERSATION 1 (with everyday expressions)

Read this conversation as you listen to the audio recording. Do you know what the _underlined_ words mean? They are colloquial or everyday expressions.

Receptionist: Good afternoon, Davison's Plumbing. _**Hold the line**_ please...
Sorry to keep you waiting. Can I help you?

Customer: Yes. Is that Davison's Plumbing?

Receptionist: Yes, it is.

Customer: I'd like a plumber to _**take a look at**_ my toilet please. It seems to be blocked.

Receptionist: Certainly. We're a bit _**snowed under**_ this afternoon so the plumber
may not be able to _**make it**_ there until tomorrow. Is that OK?

Customer: Not really. We're _**in a fix**_ because we've only got one toilet.
Is it possible for him to come sooner?

Receptionist: Mm. It's a bit _**iffy**_, I'm sorry. He's been _**flat out**_ today but if you'd like to _**hang on**_
a minute, I'll try to _**get hold of**_ him on his mobile and see how he's _**fixed for time**_.

Customer: OK. Thankyou.

Receptionist: ....Well you're in luck. He's _**had a good run**_ with his work
today and his last appointment was _**called off,**_ so he can _**fit you in**_ at about 5 p.m.

Customer: Oh great! Could you give me some idea what I'll _**be up for**_?

Receptionist: No sorry, not until he _**sorts out**_ the cause of the problem but don't
worry he'll _**fill you in**_ on the cost before he starts work.

Customer: OK. Thanks very much for your help.

Receptionist: _**No worries**_. Could I have your name and address please?

Customer: Yes, it's Mr. Ford.

Receptionist: Sorry, I didn't _**catch**_ that. Did you say Sword?

Customer: No. Ford. F for father, - O - R - D. My address is....

Don't worry, we'll sort out the problem.

Now let's see what these expressions mean - look at the next page.

CONVERSATION 2 (explanation of everyday expressions)

Compare Conversation 1 with Conversation 2 -You will see that some of the words are different but the meaning is the same in both conversations. Find the underlined words in Conversation 1, then underline the words with the same meaning in Conversation 2. For example: *Hold the line* (Conversation 1) = *Wait a moment* (Conversation 2)

Receptionist:	Good afternoon Davison's Plumbing. <u>Wait a moment</u> please... Sorry to keep you waiting. Can I help you?
Customer:	Yes. Is that Davison's Plumbing?
Receptionist:	Yes, it is.
Customer:	I'd like a plumber to inspect my toilet please. It seems to be blocked.
Receptionist:	Certainly. We're a bit busy this afternoon so the plumber may not be able to arrive there until tomorrow. Is that OK?
Customer:	Not really. We're in a difficult situation because we've only got one toilet. Is it possible for him to come sooner?
Receptionist:	Mm. It's a bit uncertain, I'm sorry. He's been very busy today but if you'd like to wait a minute, I'll try to speak with him on his mobile (cellular) telephone and see how much (spare) time he has available.
Customer:	OK. Thankyou.
Receptionist:	.........Well you're in luck. He's made good progress with his work today and his last appointment was cancelled, so he can make time for you at about 5 p.m.
Customer:	Oh great! Could you give me some idea of what I'll have to pay?
Receptionist:	No sorry, not until he determines / finds the answer to the cause of the problem but don't worry he'll give you information on the cost before he starts work.
Customer:	OK. Thanks very much for your help.
Receptionist:	You are welcome. It is not a problem to help you. Could I have your name and address please?
Customer:	Yes, it's Mr. Ford.
Receptionist:	Sorry, I didn't hear/understand that. Did you say Sword?
Customer:	No. Ford. F for father, - O - R - D. My address is....

> **Now to become familiar with the everyday expressions, practise reading CONVERSATION 1 aloud with a partner.**

Listen to the conversation again and fill in the missing words. You may have to listen more than once. (Don't worry about your spelling as this exercise focuses on listening skills - you can check your spelling later.)

Receptionist: Good afternoon, Davison's Plumbing. ***Hold the*** _____ please...

Sorry to keep you waiting. Can I help you?

Customer: Yes. Is that Davison's Plumbing?

Receptionist: Yes, it is.

Customer: I'd like a plumber to _____ ***a*** _____ ***at*** my toilet please. It seems to be blocked.

Receptionist: Certainly. We're a bit _____ ***under*** this afternoon so the plumber may not be able to _____ ***it*** there until tomorrow. Is that OK?

Customer: Not really. We're ***in a*** _____ because we've only got one toilet.

Is it possible for him to come sooner?

Receptionist: Mm. It's a bit _____, I'm sorry. He's been _____ ***out*** today but if you'd like to ***hang on*** a minute, I'll try to ***get*** _____ ***of*** him on his mobile and see how he's _____ ***for time***.

Customer: OK. Thankyou.

Receptionist: ....Well you're in luck. He's ***had a good*** _____ with his work today and his last appointment was ***called*** ___, so he can ***fit you*** _____ at about 5 p.m.

Customer: Oh great! Could you give me some idea what I'll ***be*** _____ ***for***?

Receptionist: No sorry, not until he ***sorts*** _____ the cause of the problem but don't worry he'll ***fill you*** _____ on the cost before he starts work.

Customer: OK. Thanks very much for your help.

Receptionist: ***No*** _____. Could I have your name and address please?

Customer: Yes, it's Mr. Ford.

Receptionist: Sorry, I didn't _____ that. Did you say Sword?

Customer: No. Ford. F for father, - O - R - D. My address is...

Now check your answers by comparing this page with CONVERSATION 1

In order to become more familiar with these new everyday expressions,

1) **Listen to Conversation 1 again and tick the boxes** ☐ **next to the expressions as you hear them.**

2) **After the conversation has finished, write in the definitions you can remember. (Some have been done for you as examples.)**

3) **Check your answers by turning to page 97.**

☐ Hold the line...

☐ take a look at.......................................*inspect*...

☐ snowed under..

☐ to make it.......................................*to arrive (at a certain time)*................................

☐ in a fix...

☐ iffy..

☐ flat out..

☐ hang on...

☐ get hold of...

☐ see how (he) is fixed for time.................*ask how much time (he) has available*................

☐ to have a good run...

☐ called off...

☐ fit (someone) in...

☐ to be up for ....

☐ sort out...*find the answer to the cause of a problem*...........

☐ fill (someone) in..

☐ No worries..

☐ catch...

LANGUAGE NOTE:
"No Worries" is a friendly Australian expression that is used after someone says "Thank you." and means, "You are welcome. It was no trouble to help you."

LANGUAGE REVIEW

Now complete these sentences by choosing the appropriate expressions from the box below. You can use your reference list (previous page) to help you.

fill me in	**sort out**	**be up for**	**called off**	**make it**	**having a good run**
catch	**fit you in**	**Hang on**	**in a fix**	**snowed under**	**take a look** **iffy**

1) Could you _____ _ _____ at my car please. It's making a strange noise. (inspect)

2) I'll be home late tonight because we're _____ _____ at the office. (very busy)

3) I won't be able to _____ ____ until 9 o' clock as the trains are late. (arrive)

4) I am ____ __ _____ at the moment because I haven't got any money to pay my

   expenses. (a difficult situation)

5) It's a bit ____ whether the cricket will continue due to the heavy rain. (uncertain)

6) I'm coming soon. _____ ___ a minute. (wait)

7) Did you _____ what he just said? I couldn't hear him. (hear / understand)

8) We are _____ __ _____ ____ with this project. We'll be finished soon.

   (making good progress)

9) The business meeting has been _____ ___ . (cancelled)

10) I'm sorry Mrs Smith, we can't ____ _____ ___ for a haircut until

    Friday. (make time for you)

11) If we buy that house we'll ___ ___ _____ a lot of money. (have to pay)

12) Don't worry. We can _____ ____ this problem. (find the answer to)

13) Could you ____ ___ ___ on what I should do, please? (give me information)

(Answers: page 88)

FOCUS ON SPOKEN LANGUAGE
STAGES IN A PHONE REQUEST FOR SERVICE

A phone request for service usually has the following stages:

1) **Greeting and identification**
2) **Reason for the call**
3) **Negotiating (talking about) service arrangements (time and cost)**
4) **Giving name and address**
5) **Closing the conversation**

Find each of the stages in the following conversation and draw a line between each stage. The first one has been done for you. (Answers: page 88)

Receptionist: Good afternoon, Davison's Plumbing. ***Hold the line*** please............   **1**
                Sorry to keep you waiting. Can I help you?
Customer: Yes. Is that Davison's Plumbing?
Receptionist: Yes, it is.

- -

Customer: I'd like a plumber to ***take a look at*** my toilet please. It seems to be blocked.
Receptionist: Certainly. We're a bit ***snowed under*** this afternoon so the plumber
                may not be able to ***make it*** there until tomorrow. Is that OK?
Customer: Not really. We're ***in a fix*** because we've only got one toilet.
                Is it possible for him to come sooner?
Receptionist: Mm. It's a bit ***iffy***, I'm sorry. He's been ***flat out*** today but if you'd like to ***hang on***
                a minute, I'll try to ***get hold of*** him on his mobile and see how he's ***fixed***
                for time.
Customer: OK. Thankyou.
Receptionist: ....Well you're in luck. He's ***had a good run*** with his work
                today and his last appointment was ***called off,*** so he can ***fit you in*** at
                about 5 p.m.
Customer: Oh great! Could you give me some idea what I'll ***be up for***?
Receptionist: No sorry, not until he ***sorts out*** the cause of the problem but don't
                worry he'll ***fill you in*** on the cost before he starts work.
Customer: OK. Thanks very much for your help.
Receptionist: ***No worries***. Could I have your name and address please?
Customer: Yes, it's Mr. Ford.
Receptionist: Sorry, I didn't ***catch*** that. Did you say Sword.?
Customer: No. Ford. F for father,-O-R-D. My address is 4 Macarthur Street, Bobtown.
Receptionist: Could you spell the name of your suburb again please.
Customer: Yes it's B-O-B-T-O-W-N.
Receptionist: OK thanks. We'll see you this afternoon, at about 5 o'clock.
Customer: OK thanks. Bye
Receptionist: Bye.

FOCUS ON SPOKEN LANGUAGE - USING THE TELEPHONE ;
CHECKING YOU HAVE THE CORRECT NUMBER AND PLACE

Listen to the first part of Conversation 1 again and notice how quickly the receptionist says the company name. It is often difficult to hear a company name clearly on the phone when it is spoken quickly, especially if you are still learning English. Listen and notice how the customer in Conversation 1 overcame the problem by repeating the business name. eg. "Is that Davison's Plumbing?"

USING POLITE LANGUAGE WHEN REQUESTING SERVICE

In Australia, when we deal with service people such as tradespeople, shop assistants, or receptionists we use polite language when we are asking for something. For example, in Conversation 1 of this unit, the customer uses expressions such as:

"***Is it possible*** for him to come sooner?" and "***Could you*** give me some idea what I'll be up for?"

When requesting service it would sound very rude if we spoke too directly by saying: ***"Tell him to come sooner"*** or ***"Give me some idea what I'll be up for"***, as these sentences sound like commands.

Look at the following sentences and change them to a more polite form using,
"Could I.........................please." or ***" Could you.............................please"***

The first one has been done as an example

eg. Give me a bottle of Coke.   *Could I have a bottle of Coke, please?*

1) Give the manager this message.   _____

2) Show me the blue shirt there.   _____

3) Pass me a bag.   _____

(Answers, page 88)

GIVING YOUR NAME AND ADDRESS ON THE PHONE

When you phone a tradesperson, it is not necessary to give your name at the beginning of the call. You only need to give your name and address at the end of the call if you are making arrangements for a visit to your home. Notice that in Conversation 1, the receptionist asked the customer to repeat his name by saying, "Sorry, I didn't ***catch*** that." Then the customer spelt his surname slowly.

If you need to arrange a tradesperson to come to your home, it's a good idea to practise spelling your surname, street name and suburb aloud.

**Use this page to record everyday expressions that you hear
during your daily activities.**

UNIT 9

SOCIALISING AT A BARBECUE

Unit 9 - SOCIALISING AT A BARBECUE - Part 1

Australians generally enjoy barbecues, especially in the warmer months of the year, as they provide an opportunity for friends to get together informally. Have you been to an Australian barbecue? What kinds of things do people talk about if they meet for the first time at a barbecue (or any social occasion)?

Listen to this conversation between people who have just met at a barbecue. (Unit 9 on your audio recording.) The conversation contains many colloquial or everyday expressions which will be explained later in the unit - so don't worry if you don't understand every word. This time you are only listening for gist or general understanding of the conversation. As you listen, tick the correct answers below. (There may be more than one correct answer.)
When you have finished you can check your answers on page 89.

1) What are the names of the people having the conversation?

a) Len

b) James

c) Bill

d) Joe

e) Bob

2) Which topics do the men talk about?

a) the weather

b) politics

c) their children

d) their work

e) sport

f) religion

g) close surroundings

Now we'll look at the everyday expressions used in the conversation - turn to the next page.

CONVERSATION 1 (with everyday expressions)

Read this conversation as you listen to the audio recording. Do you know what the _underlined_ words mean? They are colloquial or everyday expressions.

Bill: ***G'day. How're you going***? Bill's the name.

Len: G'day Bill - I'm Len - Bob's brother.

Bill: Oh right. Pleased to meet you. Is this seat free?

Len: Yeah, sure. ***Go for your life***.

Bill: Gee, it's been ***a scorcher*** today, hasn't it.

Len: ***I reckon!***

Bill: It's cooling down now though. The trouble is, when the sun goes down the ***mozzies*** start biting.

Len: That's for sure. It's ***a top spot*** here though, isn't it. Do you live around here?

Bill: Yeah, I just live along the street. We've been here ***going on*** two years now. What about you? Are you from around here?

Len: No, we live on the other side of town. I've just been transferred to the area by the bank.

Bill: Oh right. So what do you do there?

Len: Oh, I work in the accounts department - at the moment I'm upgrading their computer systems. What line of work are you in?

Bill: I'm in the building ***game***. I'm a ***brickie***. I work with Joe and Kev over there. I'll introduce you in ***a tick***. Ready for ***a top up***?

Len: No, ***She'll be right***, thanks, mate I'll ***give it a miss*** for a while.

Bill: ***Fair enough***. There's plenty of ***stubbies*** in the esky, so help yourself if you change your mind. Mm, the ***barbie***'s starting to smell pretty good, isn't it?

Len: ***Too right!*** So how's the building game at the moment?

Bill: Oh, business has been ***slow*** over the past few months but things are starting to ***pick up*** now. In fact, I've been ***flat chat*** the last few weeks.

Len: Well, let's hope it ***keeps up*** then. By the way - have you heard how the cricket scores are going? The Aussies weren't doing too well yesterday.

Bill: No, I haven't heard. Joe might know; he's ***into*** cricket more than me. Come on, I'll introduce you.

Now let's see what these expressions mean - look at the next page.

CONVERSATION 2 (explanation of everyday expressions)

Compare Conversation 1 with Conversation 2 -You will see that some of the words are different but the meaning is the same in both conversations. Find the underlined words in Conversation 1, then underline the words with the same meaning in Conversation 2. For example: *G'day. How're you going*?(Conversation 1) = *Hello. How are you?*(Conversation 2)

Bill: <u>Hello. How are you</u>? Bill's my name.

Len: Hello Bill - I'm Len - Bob's brother.

Bill: Oh right. Pleased to meet you. Is this seat free (available)?

Len: Yes, of course. You are welcome (to have the seat.)

Bill: Gee, it's been a very hot day today, hasn't it.

Len: Yes, I agree!

Bill: It's cooling down now though. The trouble is, when the sun goes down the mosquitoes start biting.

Len: That's for sure. It's a very nice place here though, isn't it. Do you live around here?

Bill: Yes, I just live along the street.We've been here almost two years now. What about you? Are you from around here?

Len: No, we live on the other side of town. I've just been transferred to the area by the bank.

Bill: Oh right. So what do you do there?

Len: Oh, I work in the accounts department - at the moment I'm upgrading their computer systems. What line (type) of work are you in?

Bill: I'm in the building business. I'm a bricklayer. I work with Joe and Kev over there. I'll introduce you in a minute. Ready for something more to drink?

Len: No. Everything is OK, thankyou. I won't have one for a while.

Bill: I understand. There's plenty of small bottles of beer in the esky, so help yourself if you change your mind. The barbecue is starting to smell pretty good, isn't it?

Len: I agree! So how's the building business/ trade at the moment?

Bill: Oh, business has not been good over the past few months but things are starting to improve now. In fact, I've been very busy the last few weeks.

Len: Well, let's hope it continues then. By the way - have you heard how the cricket scores are going? The Aussies weren't doing too well yesterday.

Bill: No, I haven't heard. Joe might know; he's interested in cricket more than me. Come on I'll introduce you.

> Now to become familiar with the everyday expressions, practise reading CONVERSATION 1 aloud with a partner.

Listen to the conversation again and fill in the missing words. You may have to listen more than once. (Don't worry about your spelling as this exercise focuses on listening skills - you can check your spelling later.)

Bill: ***G'day. How're you*** _____? Bill's the name.

Len: G'day Bill - I'm Len - Bob's brother.

Bill: Oh right. Pleased to meet you. Is this seat free?

Len: Yeah, sure. ***Go for your*** _____.

Bill: Gee, it's been ***a*** _____ today, hasn't it.

Len: ***I reckon!***

Bill: It's cooling down now though. The trouble is, when the sun goes down the ***mozzies*** start biting.

Len: That's for sure. It's ***a*** _____ ***spot*** here though, isn't it. Do you live around here?

Bill: Yeah, I just live along the street. We've been here ***going*** ____ two years now. What about you? Are you from around here?

Len: No, we live on the other side of town. I've just been transferred to the area by the bank.

Bill: Oh right. So what do you do there?

Len: Oh, I work in the accounts department - at the moment I'm upgrading their computer systems. What line of work are you in?

Bill: I'm in the building _____. I'm a ***brickie***. I work with Joe and Kev over there. I'll introduce you in ***a*** _____. Ready for ***a top up***?

Len: No, ***She'll be right***, thanks, mate I'll _____ ***it a miss*** for a while.

Bill: ***Fair enough***. There's plenty of ***stubbies*** in the esky, so help yourself if you change your mind. Mm, the ***barbie***'s starting to smell pretty good, isn't it?

Len: ***Too*** _____***!*** So how's the building game at the moment?

Bill: Oh, business has been _____ over the past few months but things are starting to _____ ***up*** now. In fact, I've been _____ ***chat*** the last few weeks.

Len: Well, let's hope it ***keeps*** ____ then. By the way - have you heard how the cricket scores are going? The Aussies weren't doing too well yesterday.

Bill: No, I haven't heard. Joe might know; he's _____ cricket more than me. Come on, I'll introduce you.

> **Now check your answers by comparing this page with**
> **CONVERSATION 1**

In order to become more familiar with these new everyday expressions,

1) Listen to Conversation 1 again and tick the boxes ☐ next to the expressions as you hear them.
2) After the conversation has finished, write in the definitions you can remember. (Some have been done for you as examples.)
3) Check your answers by turning to page 98.

☐ G'day. How're you going?...

☐ go for your life..

☐ a scorcher..

☐ I reckon!..

☐ mozzies..*mosquitoes*...

☐ a top spot..

☐ going on.............................*almost / about / approxiamately*................................

☐ game...

☐ brickie..

☐ a tick..

☐ a top up...

☐ She'll be right..

☐ give it a miss...................*won't have something / won't participate*...................

☐ fair enough...

☐ stubbies..

☐ barbie..

☐ Too right!...

☐ slow.........................*not good / not going well (in a business situation)*..............

☐ pick up...

☐ flat chat..

☐ to keep up..

☐ to be into (something)..

LANGUAGE NOTE: "*Go for your life*" is often said after a request for a favour and means, "Of course, help yourself, you're welcome." For example: "Could I borrow your dictionary?"
"Yes of course. Go for your life."

CULTURAL NOTE: People often get to know each other by asking about their jobs.
Some ways to ask this are: What line of work are you in?
What do you do for a living?
What do you do?
What do you do *for a crust*? (very casual)

LANGUAGE REVIEW

Complete the sentences, choosing from the everyday expressions which are listed below. You can use the clues in brackets ( ) at the end of each sentence to help you. Then complete the crossword using the everyday expressions you have written. The first one has been done as an example.

mozzie	go for your life	stubbie	into	top up	barbie
	give it a miss	she'll be right	scorcher		

ACROSS

1) "Do you need any help?" "No, ___She'll be right___, thanks." (Everything is OK, thanks)
3) "We're having a _____ on Friday night. Would you like to come?" (barbecue)
5) "Could I borrow your pen for a minute please?" Of course, ___ ____ _____ _____ (You are welcome (to have the pen.)
7) I'm not _____ outdoor sports much. I prefer indoor games like chess or cards. (interested in)

DOWN

2) I've got _____ bites all over my legs and they are very itchy. (mosquito)
4) Yesterday was a _____ so I hope today will be a bit cooler. (very hot day)
6) There's only one _____ left in the fridge, so I'll buy some more tomorrow. (small bottles of beer)
8) "Would you like to come to the movies with us tonight?" "No, thanks. I'll _____ ___ __ _____, I'm very tired. (won't participate)
10) "That coffee was delicious." "Would you like a _____ ___?" (some more to drink)

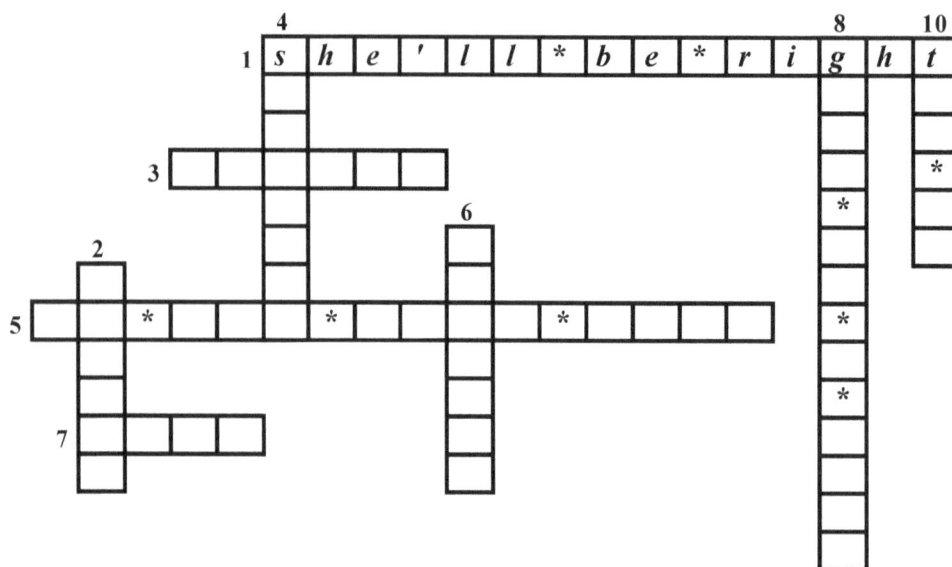

		4									8	10
1	s	h	e	'	l	l	*	b	e	*	r	i	g	h	t

(crossword grid)

(Answers: page 89)

FOCUS ON SPOKEN LANGUAGE - MAKING SMALL TALK

When we meet someone for the first time we have to think of things to talk about to be friendly and get to know the person better. This is known as "*making small talk*" and means talking about general (rather than personal) topics. Look at Conversation 1 again and notice the topics that Bill and Len talked about. Number the boxes in the order in which the topics were talked about. The first topic of conversation has been numbered for you.

☐ **the weather**   ☐ **their jobs**   ☐ **close surroundings**

☐ **sport**   ☐ **where they live**   ☐ **the barbecue**

1 **their names (who they are)**   **(Answers: page 89)**

Notice that Bill and Len talked about **general** things and were careful not to be too personal or ask questions about topics which may be considered private. For example, notice how Len asked Bill about where he lived. He asked, **"Do you live around here?"**
It was a general question so Bill didn't have to say exactly where he lived if he didn't want to.
This is an important cultural point to remember, as Australians may become offended if you ask personal questions or make personal comments. Look at the topics below and decide which are <u>*inappropriate*</u> (not suitable) questions to ask someone you have just met at a barbecue. Put a cross (X) next to the **inappropriate** questions. (Answers: page 89)

TOPIC	QUESTIONS
Job	☐ **What do you do for a living?**
	☐ **How much money do you earn?**
Family	☐ **Is your family here at the barbecue too?**
	☐ **Why don't you have any children?**
	☐ **Are you married?**
	☐ **Why aren't you married?**
Home	☐ **Have you lived in this area very long?**
	☐ **How much did your house cost?**
	☐ **What is your address?**

FOCUS ON SPOKEN LANGUAGE
INTRODUCING YOURSELF AND OTHERS IN INFORMAL SITUATIONS

Bill's greeting to Len in Conversation 1, ***"G'day. How're you going? Bill's the name"***, is more typical of an informal male greeting than female speech. Other informal forms of greeting used by both sexes are:

> *Hello. We haven't met. I'm..........*
> *Hi. How are you? My name's.................*

When we introduce ourselves to other people at informal gatherings we sometimes add extra information about ourselves to help the conversation to continue. For example, in reply to Bill's introduction, Len said, *"G'day Bill - I'm Len - **Bob's brother** "*. This helped Bill to understand more about Len and why he was at the barbecue.

PRACTICE:

Imagine that you are at the barbecue. You have just met Len and you are going to introduce him to other people. What other information about him could you include in a short introduction. Read Conversation 1 again and then complete the introduction below.

I'd like you to meet Len, Bob's brother. He's_____

_____

Answer: page 89

TURN TAKING IN CONVERSATION
Look at Conversation 1 again. You will notice that Bill and Len speak for approximately equal lengths of time rather than one person doing all the talking and the other all the listening. You will also notice that each speaker gives a little information or makes a comment, then asks a question to show interest in the other person. This in an important conversation strategy to practise when socialising. (This pattern does not apply in situations such as job interviews or doctor's consultations, where one person would be asking most of the questions and the other would be giving information.

REVISION

In this book we have focused on many strategies of spoken English, such as the use of ***contractions*** (eg. we'll, that's), ***question tags*** (eg. "It's a top spot here, isn't it?"), giving ***feedback*** (eg. Yeah, sure), using ***conversation fillers*** (eg. Mm, well...) and ***stress*** and ***intonation***, as well as expressions for ***changing the topic of the conversation*** (eg. By the way....).

Read and listen to Conversation 1 again. You will notice that almost all of these conversation strategies have been used by the speakers as they are a natural part of everyday spoken Australian

REMEMBER - THE MORE YOU LISTEN TO EVERYDAY CONVERSATIONS, THE MORE YOU WILL UNDERSTAND EVERYDAY AUSTRALIAN.

Use this page to record everyday expressions that you hear during your daily activities.

(Units 7 - 9)

This section reviews some of the expressions that were introduced in Units 7, 8, and 9 and gives you a chance to see what you have remembered.

- **Look at the pictures on the opposite page and decide what the people are saying by choosing from the expressions below.**

- **Match each picture with an appropriate expression by writing the correct letter in the box next to each expression.**

- **For extra practice, you could write the appropriate expression in the space provided in the picture.**

(Answers: page 89)

1) I'm in a fix! What am I going to do now? ☐

2) Oh no! I think I've let the cat out of the bag. ☐

3) I'm going to take it easy this afternoon. ☐

4) I'm right. I'll give it a miss thanks. ☐

5) We love it here. We have to rough it but we're in our element. ☐

6) Ready for a top up? ☐

7) Of course. Go for your life. ☐

8) We're snowed under here at the office so I'll be home late. ☐

9) Sorry I didn't catch that. It's a bit noisy in here. ☐

PART - 1

1) a) her new job
2) b) a computer course
3) a) he is too old to learn new things, & c) he will enquire about a course this week

PART - 5 CROSSWORD

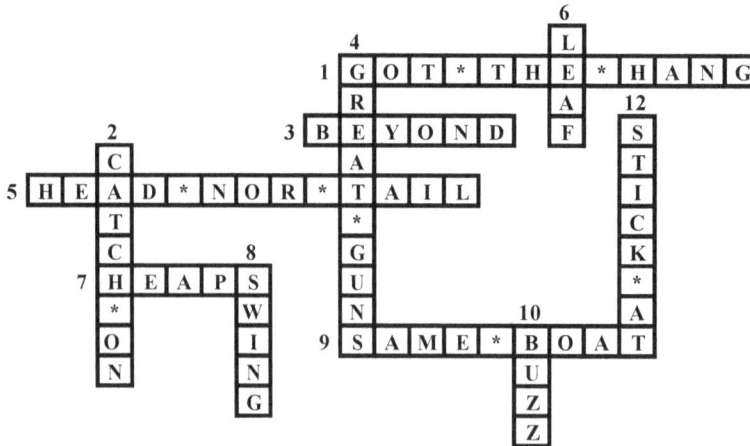

PART - 6 FOCUS ON SPOKEN LANGUAGE

There are 23 contractions in Conversation 1

PRACTICE

I am	= I'm
I have	= I've
could not	= couldn't
do not	= don't
have not	= haven't
they will	= they'll
you have	= you've
I had	= I'd
they are	= they're

PART - 1

They are talking about the first photo, which is a photo of Jane's two sons.

1) a) two
2) c) a heart problem
3) b) cultural differences

PART - 5 CROSSWORD

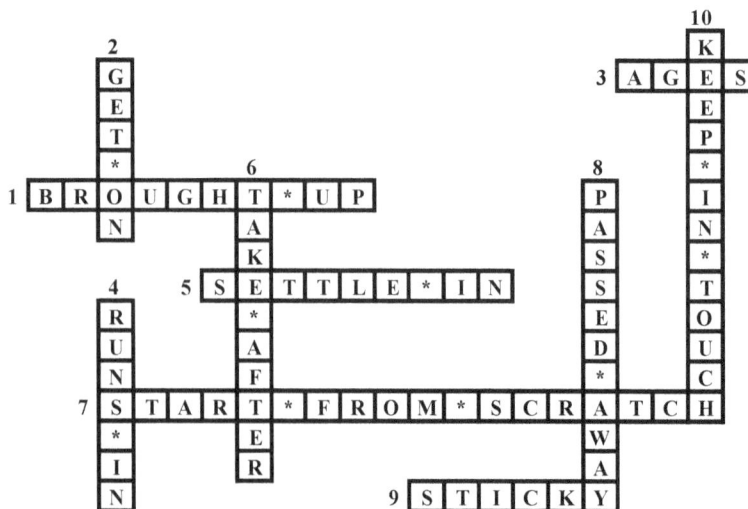

PART - 6   FOCUS ON SPOKEN LANGUAGE

1) He's the image of his father isn't he?	Yes, he is.
2) He wasn't very old, was he?	No, he wasn't - only 34.
3) In-laws can be a problem sometimes, can't they?	Yes, they can sometimes.

a) Cars can be expensive, can't they?	Yes, they can.
b) It's cold today, isn't it?	Yes, it is.
c) This classroom isn't very big. is it?	No, it isn't.
d) This food is delicious, isn't it?	Yes, it is.

ANSWERS TO UNIT THREE - TALKING ABOUT THE NEIGHBOURS

PART - 1
1) b) not very happy
2) c) likes her neighbours on one side of her house but doesn't like the neighbours on the other side.
3) a) he hasn't met his new neighbours yet.
4) c) is probably watching Bob and her.

PART - 5   CROSSWORD

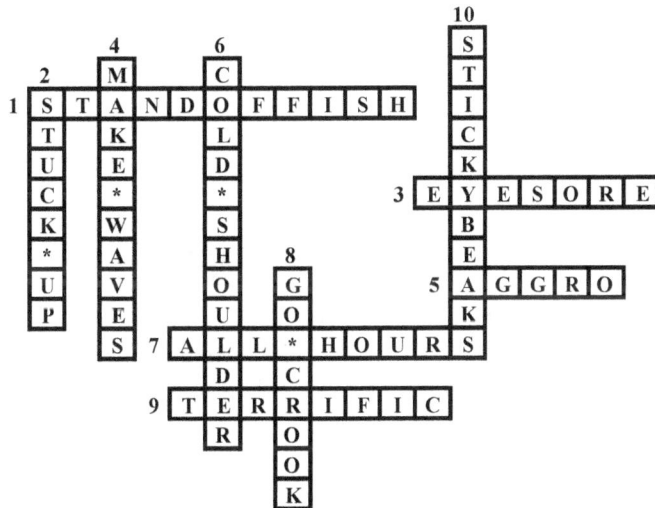

PART - 6   FOCUS ON SPOKEN LANGUAGE

CHANGING THE TOPIC
By the way, how are your new neighbours Bob?

GIVING AN OPINION
So I think they're stuck up, if you ask me.

LANGUAGE REVIEW ONE

1) F	4) H	7) C
2) D	5) I	8) B
3) A	6) E	9) G

ANSWERS TO UNIT FOUR - TALKING ABOUT SHOPPING

PART - 1
1) b) a pair of shoes
2) a) before they start shopping
3) a) both enjoy shopping
4) b) 2 o' clock

PART - 5   CROSSWORD

```
                                                              8
                                                              B
        2                    4                 6              R
    1 C U P P A       3 L O S E * T R A C K     O
        U                    P                 H     K
    5 S T I C K Y B E A K          7 V E G I E S
        H                    N                 C
        E                    D                 K
    9 D E L I 11 P R I C E Y      *
                             N                 O
              12             G                 U
              R             *                 T
        10    P             P
    13 C H R I S S I E      R
        O    *             E
        Z    O             E
        Z    F
        I    F
        E
```

PART - 6   FOCUS ON SPOKEN LANGUAGE

A) 16 contractions

B)

Statement	Question tag	Reply
1) Some shoes are a rip-off,	aren't they?	(No reply)
2) You won't get carried away with your shopping and lose track of time,	will you?	Don't worry, I won't.

C) By the way you should check out the dress shop next to the chemist for your going out gear.

ANSWERS TO UNIT FIVE - VISITING THE DOCTOR

PART - 1 diarrhoea   - a sickness which causes frequent visits to the toilet
symptoms   - signs or changes to the health of a person
prescription - a doctor's written instruction for the use of medicine
examination - a careful inspection

1) c) her son is sick & d) she feels unwell   2) b) a headache
3) b) have a few days off work

PART - 5   CROSSWORD

```
                                           6
                        2     4            O
        1 P U T T I N G * I T * O N
                 10        C     H         *
        8    3 O F F * C O L O U R         T
        W         I     M     O            H
        A         T     E     W            E
        S         *     *     *            *
        H         A     D     U            M
    5 T H E * R U N S   O     P            E
    12   D   *   *      W                  N
    K    *   O   A      N
    E    7 P I C K * U P *
    E    *   T   F      W
    *   A       I      I
    A         D      T
    N         D      H
    *         L
    E     9 C O M E * U P * W I T H
    Y
  11 T A K E * I T * E A S Y
        *
    13 C R O O K
        N
```

PART - 6   FOCUS ON SPOKEN LANGUAGE

Doctor:	What seems to be the problem, Mrs Smith?	1
Mrs. Smith	Well actually, it's my son. He's been *off colour* since yesterday. At first I thought he was *putting it on* because he didn't want to go to school but then he started *throwing up* and he's had *the runs* as well. He's *picked up* a lot today but he still seems to be a bit *washed out.*	2
Doctor	Mm. He's probably got the *bug* that's going around.	4
	Pop him on the table and I'll give him a *check up.* Has he complained about a sore *tummy?*	3
Mrs. Smith	He did yesterday - not so much today	
Doctor:	Mm. Just *keep an eye on* him. I'll give you a prescription for some medicine but I think he's *on the mend.*	5
	Is there anything else?	1
Mrs. Smith	Yes. Could you *take a look at* me while I'm here? I think I'm coming *down with something.* Usually I'm *as fit as a fiddle* but the last couple of days I've been feeling really *crook.*	2
Doctor:	Mm. It could be the same bug....	4
	Any other symptoms?	1
Mrs. Smith	Yes. I feel really *washed out* and I've had *a splitting headache.*	2
Doctor:	And when did these symptoms *come on?*	
Mrs. Smith	About five days ago...but I've been having bad headaches for a while now.	
Doctor:	Mm. Have you been *overdoing it* lately? Are you worrying about something?	
Mrs. Smith	I suppose I am *a worrywart* and I've been *pretty uptight* lately about work at the office.	
Doctor	Well first of all, I think you need a few days off work to take it easy. If the problem doesn't *clear up* in a few days we'll run some tests and see what we *come up with.*	5
Mrs. Smith	OK. Thankyou Doctor.	6

ANSWERS TO UNIT SIX - WORRYING ABOUT MONEY

PART - 1

1) b) at home

2) a) household bills

3) b) have similar opinions

PART - 5   CROSSWORD

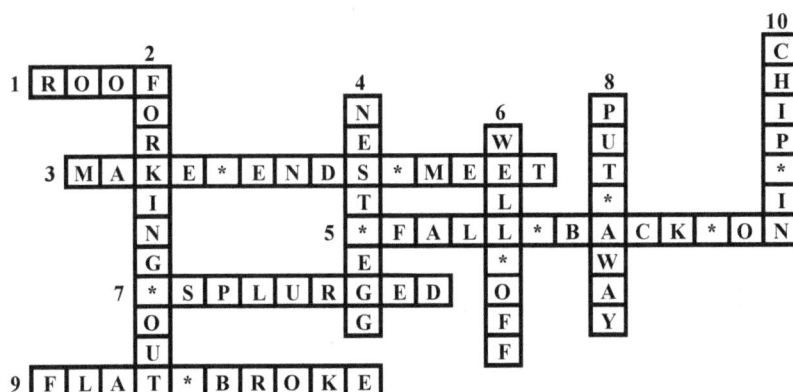

```
                                                    10
                                                    [C]
        2                                           [H]
1 [R][O][O][F]        4              8              [I]
        [O]          [N]            [P]             [P]
        [R]          [E]     6      [U]             [*]
3 [M][A][K][E][*][E][N][D][S][*][M][E][E][T]        [I]
        [I]          [T]     [W]    [*]             [N]
        [N]    5   [*][F][A][L][L][*][B][A][C][K][*][O][N]
        [G]          [E]     [*]    [W]
    7 [*][S][P][L][U][R][G][E][D]   [A]
        [O]          [G]     [O]    [Y]
        [U]                  [F]
9 [F][L][A][T][*][B][R][O][K][E][F]
```

PART - 6 FOCUS ON SPOKEN LANGUAGE

We could ask them to chip in for the phone bill, _seeing they're the ones who are on the phone for hours_, chatting to their friends.

He thinks they should chip in for part of the phone bill _seeing they've both got part-time jobs._

LANGUAGE REVIEW TWO

1) D	4) I	7) A
2) H	5) C	8) F
3) B	6) E	9) G

ANSWERS TO UNIT SEVEN - TALKING ABOUT HOLIDAYS

PART - 1

A) camping, remote

B) resort, luxury

1) b) at work
2) b) their ideas about future holidays
3) b) a year
4) a) have different ideas about holidays

PART - 5   REVISION EXERCISES

1) off the beaten track
2) a send-off
3) in my element
4) rat race
5) take it easy
6) rough it
7) spilled the beans
8) drives me up the wall
9) cup of tea

PART - 6 FOCUS ON SPOKEN LANGUAGE

John: I'm glad it's Friday. Bye Susan, I'll see you on Monday.

Susan: Monday? I'll see you at your send-off tomorrow night.

John: Send-off? I thought I was going to Peter's house for dinner..... So they're having a send off for me, are they?

Susan: Oh dear. I think I've let the cat out of the bag. But nobody told me to keep it hush hush.

John: Don't worry. I won't tell anyone you spilled the beans. It'll be fun!

Susan: Oh good..... I hear that you're taking a year off work to travel. Where are you planning to go?

John: Well, I want to see as much of the world as possible but I want to get off the beaten track and away from the rat race of city life. I plan to visit the outback of Australia first.

Susan: Well, it sounds like you'll be on the go.

John: Oh yes, and I'll have to rough it but I'll be in my element! I love camping and going bush!

Susan: Really?..... Well, that's not for me. I'd prefer to live it up at a resort where I'd be waited on hand and foot. Somewhere I could let my hair down, party at night and then take it easy beside the pool during the day.

John: Oh no. . .It would drive me up the wall to lie around a pool all day. That's not my cup of tea at all.

Susan: Oh well, to each his own. I'll see you on Saturday anyway. And please don't tell anyone I let the cat out of the bag.

John: Don't worry, I won't.

PART - 1

1) b) a plumber
2) b) 5 p.m.
3) a) Mr. Ford

PART - 5   LANGUAGE REVIEW

1) take a look
2) snowed under
3) make it
4) in a fix
5) iffy
6) Hang on
7) catch

8) having a good run
9) called off
10) fit you in
11) be up for
12) sort out
13) fill me in

PART 6 - STAGES IN A PHONE REQUEST FOR SERVICE

Receptionist:	Good afternoon, Davison's Plumbing. ***Hold the line*** please.....................	1
	Sorry to keep you waiting. Can I help you?	
Customer:	Yes. Is that Davison's Plumbing?	
Receptionist:	Yes, it is.	
Customer:	I'd like a plumber to ***take a look at*** my toilet please. It seems to be blocked.	2
Receptionist:	Certainly. We're a bit ***snowed under*** this afternoon so the plumber	
	may not be able to ***make it*** there until tomorrow. Is that OK?	
Customer:	Not really. We're ***in a fix*** because we've only got one toilet.	
	Is it possible for him to come sooner?	
Receptionist:	Mm. It's a bit ***iffy***, I'm sorry. He's been ***flat out*** today but if you'd like to ***hang on***	
	a minute, I'll try to ***get hold of*** him on his mobile and see how he's ***fixed for time***.	
Customer:	OK. Thankyou.	3
Receptionist:	.........Well you're in luck. He's ***had a good run*** with his work	
	today and his last appointment was ***called off***, so he can ***fit you in*** at	
	about 5 p.m.	
Customer:	Oh Great! Could you give me some idea what I'll ***be up for***?	
Receptionist:	No sorry, not until he ***sorts out*** the cause of the problem but don't	
	worry he'll ***fill you in*** on the cost before he starts work.	
Customer:	OK. Thanks very much for your help.	
Receptionist:	***No worries***. Could I have your name and address please?	
Customer:	Yes, it's Mr. Ford.	
Receptionist:	Sorry, I didn't ***catch*** that. Did you say Sword.?	
Customer:	No. Ford. F for father, - O - R - D. My address is 4 Macarthur Street, Bobtown.	
Receptionist	Could you spell the name of your suburb again please.	
Customer:	Yes it's B-O-B-T-O-W-N.	4
Receptionist:	OK thanks. We'll see you this afternoon, at about 5 o' clock.	
Customer:	OK thanks. Bye	5
Receptionist:	Bye.	

USING POLITE LANGUAGE WHEN REQUESTING SERVICE

1) Could you give the manager this message, please?
2) Could you show me the blue shirt there, please?
3) Could you pass me a bag, please?

PART - 1

1) a) Len & c) Bill
2) a) the weather, d) their work, e) sport, g) close surroundings (nearby area)

PART - 5   CROSSWORD

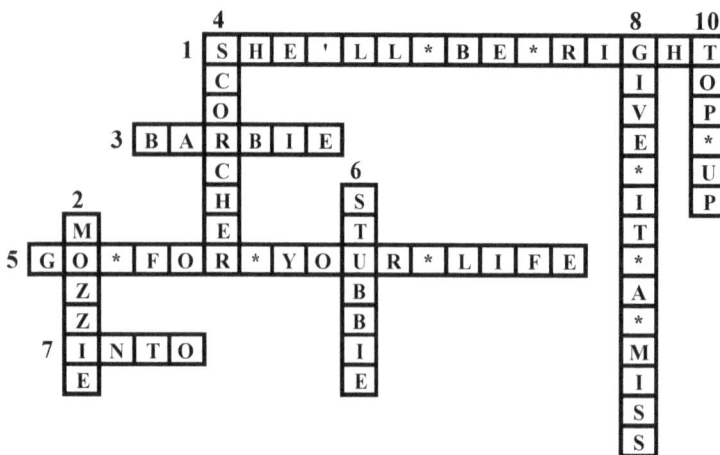

```
                    4                               8    10
            1  S  H  E  '  L  L  *  B  E  *  R  I  G  H  T
               C                                  I     O
               O                                  V     P
         3  B  A  R  B  I  E                       E     *
               C              6                    *     U
         2     H              S                    I     P
            M  E              T
         5  G  O  *  F  O  R  *  Y  O  U  R  *  L  I  F  E
            Z                 B                    T
            Z                 B                    *
         7  I  N  T  O        I                    A
            E                 E                    *
                                                   M
                                                   I
                                                   S
                                                   S
```

PART - 6   FOCUS ON SPOKEN LANGUAGE

1) their names (who they are)
2) the weather
3) close surroundings
4) where they live
5) their jobs
6) the barbecue
7) sport

Inappropriate questions

How much do you earn?
Why don't you have any children?
Are you married?
Why aren't you married?
How much did your house cost?
What is your address?

INTRODUCING YOURSELF AND OTHERS IN INFORMAL SITUATIONS

I'd like you to meet Len, Bob's brother. <u>He's just been transferred here by the bank.</u>

ANSWERS TO LANGUAGE REVIEW THREE

1) A
2) I
3) C
4) B
5) D
6) F
7) G
8) H
9) E

EVERYDAY EXPRESSIONS	*DEFINITIONS*
give (someone) a buzz..................	call (someone) on the telephone
getting on	progressing
going great guns..........................	progressing very well
hassles.......................................…	difficulties/problems
get the hang of (it)	understand what to do
beyond (someone).....................….	too difficult for (someone)
not make head or tail of............…	to **not** understand anything
stick at (something)....................	to keep trying
get into the swing of things......…	to become familiar with the usual way of doing things
Good for you! ....…	Congratulations!
What've you been up to?.............	What have you been doing?
take a leaf out of (someone's) book	copy someone's good example
not have the foggiest idea...........	have **no** knowledge about (something)
catch on.......................…...........	to learn / understand
(new) tricks...............................….....	(new) ways of doing things
Come off it!................................	I don't agree with you!
heaps..	a lot/many
in the same boat...........................	in the same situation
Go on!..	You should do it!
talk into (something)....................	show good reasons (for doing something)
Catch you later!...........................	Goodbye
Hooroo......................................…	Goodbye

EVERYDAY EXPRESSIONS	*DEFINITIONS*
for ages..	for a long time
the image of (someone).................	the same in appearance
take after.......................................	to be similar to (an older family member)
I reckon!.......................................	I agree!
follow in (someone's) footsteps.....	do the same as someone has done before/ to copy someone's example
start from scratch..........................	start from the beginning without help
be settled in...................…..........	become established (in a new place)
give (someone) my best...............	give (someone) my best wishes
runs in the family...............…......	is a common family characteristic
fair dinkum?.................................	really?
passed away.................…..........	died
keep in touch..............…...........	communicate regularly
be very close.................................	have a good relationship
not get on......................................	not have a good relationship
sticky...................................…......	difficult
a tough one..................…..........	a difficult problem
bring up (children)........................	train and educate (within the family)
get on with...................…...........	be friendly with
rub off on...................…......	transfer (a habit, idea) to another person

TALKING ABOUT THE NEIGHBOURS - REFERENCE LIST

EVERYDAY EXPRESSIONS	*DEFINITIONS*
out of sorts.................................	unhappy
not sleep a wink..........................	not sleep at all
a racket......................................	a lot of noise
all hours.....................................	very late at night
couldn't care less........................	don't care at all
fed up...	unhappy, discontented
go crook on.................................	tell (someone) you are displeased with them
make waves.................................	cause trouble
stroppy..	angry, difficult to deal with
aggro..	aggressive
wayout..	strange/unusual
an eyesore...................................	an unpleasant thing / place to look at
terrific..	excellent
spot on..	perfect
easy to get on with.......................	friendly
hassles..	problems
standoffish..................................	unfriendly
give (someone) the cold shoulder..	deliberately ignore (someone)
be stuck up.....................…........	snobbish / to believe you are superior to other people
a stickybeak....................…......	a person who watches what other people are doing
a busybody.....................…...….	an interfering person
going on....................................….	happening

TALKING ABOUT SHOPPING - REFERENCE LIST

EVERYDAY EXPRESSIONS	DEFINITIONS
to be a bit broke......................	to not have much money
shop around............................	visit a few shops to look for the best price
cost an arm and a leg...............	cost too much / a lot of money
a rip-off.................................	overpriced
to check out...........................	to look at/ to look in
a deli....................................	delicatessen (shop which sells cooked meat and cheese)
pricey....................................	expensive
pick up..................................	get/collect
bits and pieces........................	small items
What are you after?.................	What are you looking for?
vegies....................................	vegetables
a spending spree......................	an enjoyable time spending a lot of money
going out gear.........................	clothes for parties etc, formal clothes
undies....................................	underwear
nightie...................................	a woman's night-dress (to wear in bed)
cozzie....................................	a swimming costume (to wear when swimming)
Chrissie..................................	Christmas
(to be) pushed for.....................	to not have enough
split up..................................	go separately; not together
cuppa....................................	a cup of tea or coffee
have a stickybeak.....................	have a look at
get carried away......................	become too interested and involved
lose track of...........................	forget about

EVERYDAY EXPRESSIONS	*DEFINITIONS*
off colour............................	sick/ unwell
putting it on............................	pretending/acting
to throw up............................	to vomit
the runs............................	diarrhoea
pick up............................	improve
washed out............................	unwell/ tired/ pale
a/the bug	a virus
pop............................	put
a check up............................	a (medical) examination
tummy............................	stomach
keep an eye on............................	keep a careful watch
on the mend............................	improving in health
take a look at............................	examine
coming down with (something)	getting a sickness
fit as a fiddle............................	very healthy
to feel crook............................	to feel sick/unwell
a splitting headache..............	a very bad headache
come on............................	begin / start
overdoing it	working too hard
a worrywart............................	a person who worries too much
pretty uptight............................	quite anxious
take it easy............................	rest / relax
clear up............................	become better
come up with............................	find/discover (an answer or solution)

EVERYDAY EXPRESSIONS	DEFINITIONS
Good grief	This a shock!
go through the roof...................	reach an extreme price/ a higher cost than normal
to be up for ($$$)	to have to pay
to get ahead	to progress financially
figure out	to understand
forking out	reluctantly / unwillingly paying
work out ....…..........	plan the details
It's got me beat ….....................	I don't understand.
well off ....…............	wealthy / rich
splurge ....…...........	to spend a lot of money
not make ends meet.......…........	to be *unable* to pay expenses
who knows.......................….....	I don't know. (nobody knows)
get by.........................……	to manage in difficult circumstances
put away (money) ....……	to save (money)
a nest egg................................	savings for the future
something to fall back on....……..	a reserve of money for future use
to be flat broke.................….....	to have no money
go easy on (something)........…...	use less / spend less of (something)
chip in....................….….......	contribute some money
chatting...................................	talking informally

TALKING ABOUT HOLIDAYS - REFERENCE LIST

EVERYDAY EXPRESSIONS

a send-off...............................

let the cat out of the bag............

hush hush................................

spill the beans...........................

off the beaten track...................

the rat race...............................

outback....................................

on the go................................

to rough it..............................

in one's element.......................

go bush...................................

live it up.................................

be waited on hand and foot........

let one's hair down....................

take it easy..............................

drive (someone) up the wall.......

not my cup of tea......................

to each his own.........................

DEFINITIONS

a farewell party

reveal a secret

secret

reveal a secret

away from the populated areas

constantly busy competition of city life

remote area (of Australia)

busy

to live without basic comforts

in one's preferred situation

live close to nature

live in luxury

have all one's needs attended to

behave very informally

relax/rest

greatly irritate

not something which interests me

everyone has their own preference

PHONING A TRADESPERSON - REFERENCE LIST

EVERYDAY EXPRESSIONS

	DEFINITIONS
hold the line...............................	wait a moment
take a look at..............................	inspect / examine
snowed under.............................	busy
to make it...................................	to arrive (at a certain time)
in a fix..	in a difficult situation
iffy...............................….....	uncertain
flat out........................…....	very busy
hang on.....................…...........	wait a minute
get hold of.....................…........	speak to, contact by phone
see how (someone) is fixed for time	ask how much time (someone) has available
to have a good run..................…...	to make good progress
called off...................…........	cancelled
fit (someone) in..................….....	to make time for someone
to be up for ....…........	to have to pay
sort out...................…........	find the answer to the cause of a problem
fill (someone) in.................….....	give information
No worries.................................	You are welcome. It is not a problem.
catch...........................….......	hear/understand

SOCIALISING AT A BARBECUE - REFERENCE LIST

EVERYDAY EXPRESSIONS	*DEFINITIONS*
G'day. How're you going?.........	Hello. How are you?
go for your life..........................	You are welcome (to borrow it.) Help yourself.
a scorcher...........................….....	a very hot day
I reckon!...............................…..	I agree!
mozzies..............................….....	mosquitoes
a top spot...........................….....	a very nice place
going on...............................….....	almost / about / approximately
game.......................................…..	business / trade
brickie.................................….....	bricklayer
a tick...............................….......	a minute / moment
a top up...............................……....	something more to drink
She'll be right..........................……	Everything is OK / fine.
give it a miss........................…......	won't have something /won't participate
fair enough.........................………..	I understand.
stubbies.............................….....	small bottles of beer
barbie...................................….....	barbecue
Too right!...........................……....	I agree!
slow......................................….....	not good / not going well (in a business situation)
pick up...............................…….	improve
flat chat...............................……....	very busy
to keep up..........................……....	to continue
to be into (something)...............……..	to be interested in (something) eg. a hobby

Boyer Educational Resources books and audio CDs

'Understanding Spoken English' – (books with audio CD) international editions

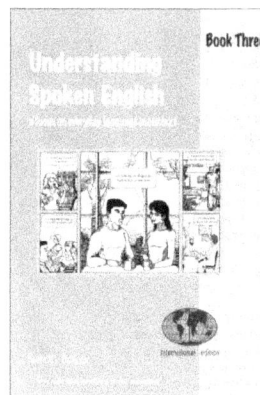

Stories, Audio CDs, Language workbooks

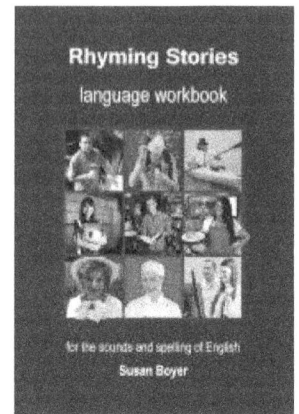

Understanding Spoken English — Book One — a focus on everyday language in context — Contains: dialogues, language reviews, answers and reference lists — Susan Boyer — Use with accompanying audio recording

Understanding Spoken English — Book Two — a focus on everyday language in context — Contains: dialogues, language reviews, answers and reference lists — Susan Boyer — Use with accompanying audio recording

Understanding Spoken English — Book Three — International edition

Rhyming Stories — language workbook — for the sounds and spelling of English — Susan Boyer

'Understanding Everyday Australian' – series (books with audio CD)

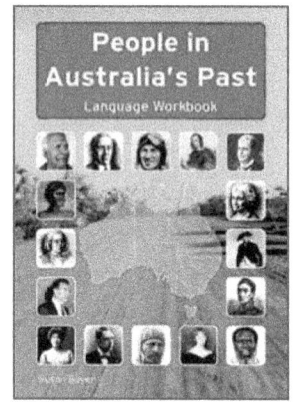

Book One — **UNDERSTANDING Everyday Australian** — A focus on spoken language with language reviews, exercises and answers — To be used with audio cassette — © Susan Boyer

Book Two — **UNDERSTANDING Everyday Australian** — A focus on spoken language with language reviews, exercises and answers — To be used with audio cassette — © Susan Boyer

Book Three — **UNDERSTANDING Everyday Australian** — A focus on spoken language with language reviews, exercises and answers — To be used with audio recording — Susan Boyer

People in Australia's Past — Language Workbook

Spelling and Pronunciation for English Language Learners	Understanding English Pronunciation	Word Building Activities for beginners of English	English Language Skills Level One

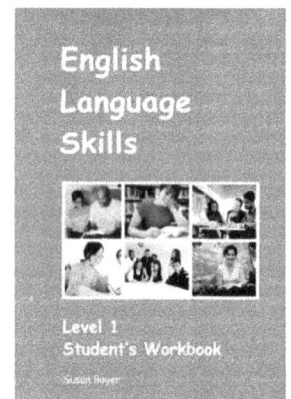

Spelling and Pronunciation for English Language Learners — SPELL — Susan Boyer — Practice Book

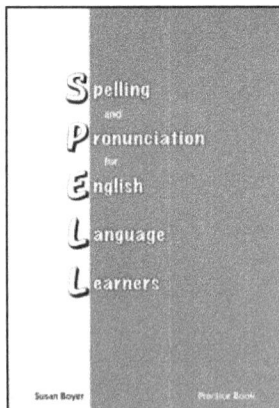

UNDERSTANDING English Pronunciation — An integrated practice course — To be used with accompanying audio recording — © Susan Boyer

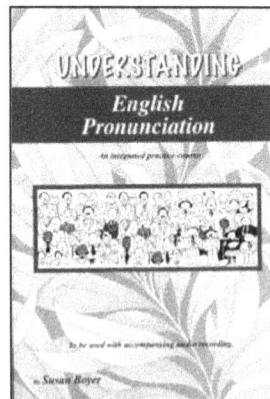

Word Building Activities — for beginners of English — Susan Boyer

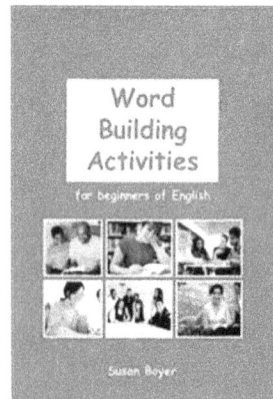

English Language Skills — Level 1 Student's Workbook — Susan Boyer

Spiral bound Teacher's Books with photocopiable activities such as surveys, role-cards & vocabulary activities:

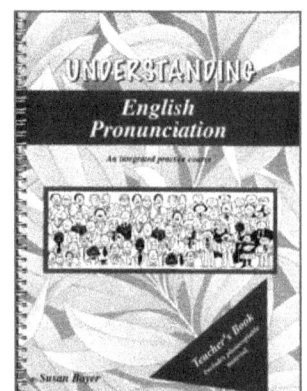

Book Two — **UNDERSTANDING Everyday Australian** — A focus on spoken language with communicative activities to enhance learning and promote classroom interaction — Susan Boyer — Teacher's Book

English Language Skills — Level 1 Teacher's Book — Susan Boyer

Understanding Spoken English — Teacher's Book Three — Teacher's photocopiable activities for classroom interaction — Susan Boyer — International edition

UNDERSTANDING English Pronunciation — An integrated practice course — Susan Boyer — Teacher's Book

All teacher's books are A4 size. Student's books contain language exercises and answers.

www.boyereducation.com.au

Boyer Educational Resources

Office phone/fax: +61 (0)2 4739 1538

e-mail: boyer@eftel.net.au

websites: www.boyereducation.com.au

www.englishebooks.com

	Title	ISBN	RRP
Focus on Australian content	People in Australia's past - language workbook A4 (156 pages)	978 1 877074 36 3	$44.95
	People in Australia's past - audio CD	978 1 877074 35 6	$19.95
	Understanding Everyday Australian - Book One	978 0 958539 50 0	$29.95
	Understanding Everyday Australian - Audio CD One (1)	978 1 877074 01 1	$19.95
	Understanding Everyday Australian - Teacher's Book One	978 0 958539 52 4	$44.95
	Understanding Everyday Australian - Book One & Audio CD	**978 1 877074 16 5**	**$39.95**
	Understanding Everyday Australian - Book Two	978 0 958539 53 1	$29.95
	Understanding Everyday Australian - Audio CD Two (1)	978 1 877074 02 8	$19.95
	Understanding Everyday Australian - Teacher's Book Two	978 0 958539 55 5	$44.95
	Understanding Everyday Australian - Book Two & Audio CD Pack	**978 1 877074 17 2**	**$39.95**
	Understanding Everyday Australian - Book Three	978 1 877074 20 2	$29.95
	Understanding Everyday Australian - Audio CD Three	978 1 877074 21 9	$19.95
	Understanding Everyday Australian - Teacher's Book Three	978 1 877074 22 6	$44.95
	Understanding Everyday Australian - Book Three & Audio CD	**978 1 877074 23 3**	**$39.95**
Beginner English	Word Building Activities for Beginners of English	978 1 877074 28 8	$29.95
	English Language Skills - Level One Student's Workbook	978 1 877074 29 5	$19.95
	English Language Skills - Level One Audio CD	978 1 877074 31 8	$19.95
	English Language Skills - Level One Teacher's Book	978 1 877074 32 5	$49.95
	English Language Skills - Level 1 Teacher's Book & Audio CD	978 1 877074 33 2	$59.95
Pronunciation & Spelling	Rhyming Stories - practice with the sounds and spelling of English (A5)	978 1 877074 06 6	$19.95
	Rhyming Stories -audio CD	978 1 877074 37 0	$19.95
	Rhyming Stories - language workbook (A4)	978 1 877074 38 7	$29.95
	English Vowel Sound Spelling Charts - A4 colour laminated & reusable	978 1 877074 39 4	$39.95
	Phonemic Charts - 2 x A3 Laminated - Vowel and Consonant	978 1 877074 05 9	$16.95
	Spelling and Pronunciation for English Language Learners	978 1 877074 04 2	$19.95
	Understanding English Pronunciation - Student book only	978 0 958539 57 9	$29.95
	Understanding English Pronunciation - Audio CD (Set of 3)	978 1 877074 03 5	$39.95
	Understanding English Pronunciation - Teacher's Book	978 0 958539 59 3	$44.95
Focus on 'International English'	Understanding Spoken English - Book One	978 1 877074 08 0	$29.95
	Understanding Spoken English - Audio CD One (1)	978 1 877074 10 3	$19.95
	Understanding Spoken English - Teacher's Book One	978 1 877074 11 0	$44.95
	Understanding Spoken English - Book One & Audio CD	**978 1 877074 18 9**	**$39.95**
	Understanding Spoken English - Book Two	978 1 877074 12 7	$29.95
	Understanding Spoken English - Audio CD Two (1)	978 1 877074 14 1	$19.95
	Understanding Spoken English - Teacher's Book Two	978 1 877074 15 8	$44.95
	Understanding Spoken English - Book Two & Audio CD	**978 1 877074 19 6**	**$39.95**
	Understanding Spoken English - Book Three	978 1 877074 24 0	$29.95
	Understanding Spoken English - Audio CD Three	978 1 877074 25 7	$19.95
	Understanding Spoken English - Teacher's Book Three	978 1 877074 26 4	$44.95
	Understanding Spoken English - Book Three & Audio CD	**978 1 877074 27 1**	**$39.95**

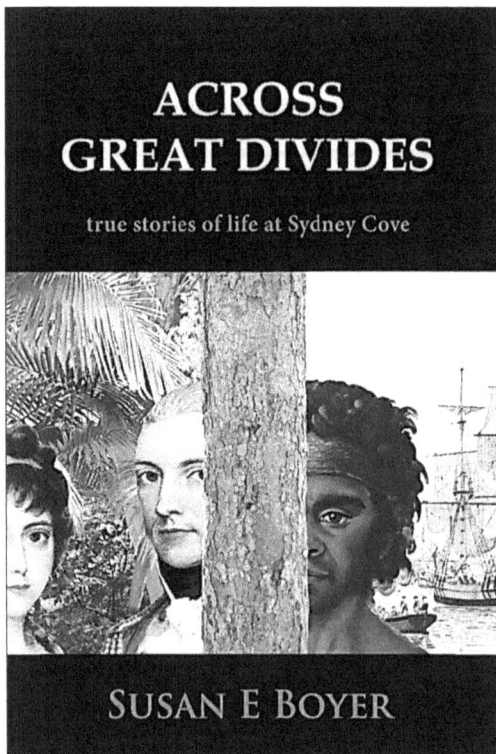

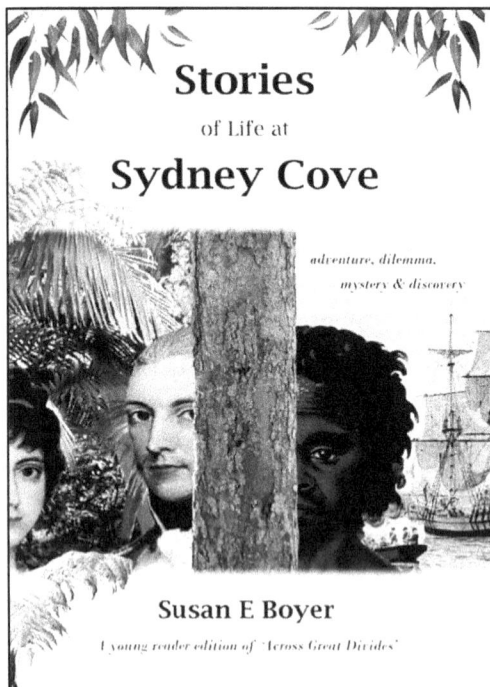

Information below sourced from **Australian Curriculum** History Units Content:

Year 4 - First contacts

* Stories of the First Fleet: who travelled to Australia; reasons for the journey: their experiences following arrival (ACHASSK085)
* Contact between Aboriginal people & Europeans, & the effects of interactions on families and the environment (ACHASSK086)

Year 5 - The Australian Colonies

* The nature of convict or colonial presence; factors that influenced patterns of development, aspects of the daily life of the inhabitants including Aboriginal Peoples and how the environment changed (ACHASSK107)
• What do we know about the lives of people in Australia's colonial past and how do we know?
• How did colonial settlement change the environment? What were the significant events & people that shaped Australia?

Year 9 - The Making of the Modern World

The nature & extent of movement of peoples in the period (convicts & settlers) (ACOKFH015)
Depth study: Movement of peoples (1750 – 1901)

• The experiences of…convicts & free settlers upon departure, their journey abroad, and their reactions on arrival, including the Australian experience (ACDSEH083)

www.ingramcontent.com/pod-product-compliance
Lightning Source LLC
Chambersburg PA
CBHW081137090426
42742CB00015BA/2869